PREA
ALI

PREACHING FOR ALL SEASONS

JOHN VIPOND

MOWBRAY

Mowbray
A Cassell imprint
Villiers House, 41/47 Strand, London WC2N 5JE

First published 1993

British Library Cataloguing-in-Publication Data
A catalogue record for this book is available from the British Library.

ISBN 0-264-67324-7

Typeset by Colset Pte Ltd, Singapore
Printed and bound in Great Britain by
Biddles Ltd, Guildford and King's Lynn

CONTENTS

FOREWORD

This book represents preaching for the ordinary parish congregation at its best. Would that there was more of it. What are the ingredients? First and foremost, there is a lively personal faith in Christ on the part of the preacher—it shines through. Secondly, the author has a love of the Bible, not least for its stories: together with competence in matters of scholarship. Thirdly, he shows sensitivity to the problematical conditions of modern living, but with an avoidance of political solutions. Fourthly, a lightness of touch is made arresting, time and time again with apt illustrations taken sometimes from the preacher's own experience. Fifthly, his language-style is free of clichés and slipshod structures. Sixthly, he gives a positive message, without dogmatism or narrowness: even if, perhaps in places, it might seem a little 'too simple' for some!

Clergy and ministers, especially those responsible for a regular preaching ministry, would be wise to have this resource-book on their shelves.

D.W. CLEVERLEY FORD

(Canon D.W. Cleverley Ford BD MTh was formerly the Hon. Director of the College of Preachers, appointed by Archbishop Coggan to help and encourage the clergy in their attempts to improve their preaching.)

PREFACE

A few centuries before the birth of Christ, in an age of doubt and cynicism, when all human experience was judged to be 'vanity' and empty of purpose, a man of faith set himself to nail the lie. The writings of this man, who called himself 'The Preacher', have a timeless appeal. Great was the excitement when portions of his manuscripts were found among the Dead Sea Scrolls, published in 1954! His thoughts ranged over all the varied seasons of life, with all their joys and sorrows. He concluded that all life, so far from being futile, finds fulfilment in the divine purpose of the Creator. 'To everything there is a season, and a time to every purpose under the heaven' (Ecclesiastes 3.1). Those who leave God out of their reckoning, may find in life nothing but travail, vanity, and vexation of spirit; but the man of faith will find in God wisdom, knowledge, and joy, he said.

Preaching for All Seasons owes its title to the unnamed author of Ecclesiastes, who so long ago 'gave good heed, and sought out, and set in order that which was upright, even words of truth' (12.9–10), expressed with a loveliness of language that will last as long as life itself.

This present little book is a humble attempt to bring faith to bear on all the changing scenes of modern life. In general, it follows the outline of the Christian year; and the meditations are Bible-based, although not restricted to the lessons appointed to be read on each Sunday. This has the advantage on the one hand of allowing freedom to express thoughts of God over a range of contemporary life-situations; and, on the other hand, providing a yearly framework of meditation, enriched by the prayers and thoughts of godly men and women down the ages.

Although these chapters have taken the shape of sermons, due to the habit of a lifetime, yet my primary intention was not to produce a book of sermons, but rather a bedtime book of meditations. The

aim was to be helpful to laity and clergy alike. I hope it may bring
both comfort and encouragement to any reader who feels the stress
and bewilderment of modern life.

JOHN VIPOND

Scripture quotations are from the Authorized Version, unless otherwise stated.

To John, David, and Paul, our sons, whom we dearly love, and pray that they may continue to 'grow in grace and in the knowledge of our Lord Jesus Christ', whom to know is life eternal (cf. 2 Peter 3.18).

ADVENT
When God Calls 'Time!'

When the fulness of the time was come, God sent forth his Son.

GALATIANS 4.4

THEN AND NOW

Today is Advent Sunday, the start of the Christian year, four weeks before Christmas. So critically important was the timing of Christmas, that men recalculated their calendars and diaries from the year Jesus was born. Every event had to be dated BC or AD, when men took account of God's time. We study the timing of Christ's first coming, lest we be caught unprepared at his *second advent*, at the climax of history when 'He shall come again in his glorious majesty to judge both the quick and the dead' (see 2 Timothy 4.1). The gospel appointed to be read on Advent Sunday tells of a time unexpected, when 'On earth nations will stand helpless, not knowing which way to turn . . . and men will faint with terror at the thought of all that is coming upon the world' (Luke 21.25, NEB). Unexpected—yet, if the conditions prevailing in the modern world were compared with conditions at Christ's *first advent*, we would realize that the world is now ripe for Christ's promised return. William Shakespeare spoke of 'a tide in the affairs of men'; and it is when the tide is full and the condition of the world cries out for God to intervene, that he will send forth his Son to save and judge. Bible students comparing the condition of the world, then and now, are becoming increasingly convinced that the time is drawing near and that once more it is 'the fulness of time'. The tide of history is rising and is almost 'at the full'. Bible students, discerning 'the signs of the times', are convinced that once again it is 'the fulness of time'. *Time* magazine, *Newsweek*, and world television, as well as the Scriptures, should alert us to the closeness of Christ's return.

1

1. THE TIDE WAS FULL

God measures time not by human clocks, but by world events. He reaps when conditions are ripe. Long centuries passed, as men count time, and Israel waited with desperate impatience for the Christ to come and deliver their nation. Scripture, however, speaks of the patience of God with whom a thousand years is but a day! God was waiting for the right time. He waited upon world events. The tide of history was rising, but not until it was full did God send forth his Son to launch the ship of salvation. Then, in the fulness of time, God sent forth his Son. God's hour struck when conditions were ready. Christ came when the world stage was set, with emperors and high priests waiting in the wings. Then, at the world's hour of destiny, the Saviour of the world came forth. Born in a stable, he was every inch a king, as befits 'great David's greater Son'. The Babe of Bethlehem was, indeed, 'The Man born to be King!' His birth date was given an imperial setting:

> In the fifteenth year of the reign of Tiberius Caesar, Pontius Pilate being governor of Judaea, and Herod being tetrarch of Galilee . . . the word of God came unto John. . . . prepare ye the way of the Lord. (Luke 3.1–4)

2. THE WORLD WAS ONE

On reading the history of the world one can only marvel at the precision of God's timing. The world was prepared, and the signs propitious. Roman legions had brought law and order. Enforced peace prevailed throughout the vast Empire. Unruly tribes were kept under firm control; brigands were driven into the hills and pirates were swept from the seas. Traders could sail unmolested through the Mediterranean Sea, and travel along fine Roman roads to every part of of the known world. For the first time in many centuries the world had opened up. Communications were good, and along the roads could travel not only the imperial messengers but also the apostles of Christ. Roman legions had pushed back the boundaries of hostile lands, and broken the barriers which centuries earlier would have blocked the advance of the Gospel. The Bible says that God can make even the wrath of men turn to his praise. Well! He certainly used the conquests of Alexander the Great to spread the Greek language! By the time the Gospel was ready to be proclaimed there was a world language ready to carry it. No language barriers could hinder the spread of the Good News, for the nations had become bilingual. The Roman Peace, the Roman roads, and the Greek language, had turned the world of the first century into one vast parish of evangelistic opportunity. Moreover, the Jewish dispersion had provided synagogues in every city, ready-made pulpits for the proclamation of the Gospel of Christ. Never before in the history of the world had there been a more propitious time for the coming of Christ and the launching of his Church. The conditions of the world cried out for deliverance; and in the fulness of time God sent forth his Son to save it.

3. THE NEED WAS GREAT

Everywhere people sat in darkness and in the shadow of death. In Rome, two out of every three were slaves; and every conquest produced more men, women, and children, to be bought and sold like cattle! They were beaten at will, and worked to death. Even the so-called 'free men' often fared little better. Soldiers, having left their farms for service abroad, returned to find their farms ruined by years of neglect, or taken over by the rich. They were faced with the option of working as labourers on the land they had once owned, or trying to make a life in the city slums. Meanwhile, the favoured rich lived sumptuously and sinfully behind the guarded walls of their town houses and country villas, their expenses being paid out of the exorbitant taxes levied on the poor.

> There lived millions upon millions of poor and tired human beings, toiling like ants who built a nest under a heavy stone. They worked for the benefit of someone else. They shared their food with the animals of the fields. They lived in stables, and died without hope. (Willem and Loon)

As for religion—the old gods of Greek myth and Roman legend were dead. To fill the 'god-gap', returning soldiers from the east brought back so many 'gods' that they packed the Pantheon. The Emperor even declared himself a god, demanding due worship from all his subjects! But what comfort can such 'gods' give to broken hearts and guilty consciences? Moral corruption and cynicism spread from palace to people. Public standards of morality and honourable behaviour were abandoned. The degenerate Emperor and his subjects sank deeper and deeper into sin. They were, indeed, 'without God, and without hope in the world'. Never was there a time more in need of the Saviour.

4. THE PROSPECT WAS DARK

It was midnight for mankind, and a time of dark despair. Then God's clock struck twelve! A new day was born. It was the fulness of time, and God sent forth his Son, to be born of a woman. On the very day that Caesar signed his heartless decree that all the world should be taxed, God sent forth his Son to save it. A new era had begun, and a new benchmark of history made. It was *anno Domini*—the year of our Lord! All that had happened before, or since, is counted, not from the foundation of Rome, but from the nativity of Christ. It was Christmas Day!

WATCHING IN HOPE

Such were the conditions preceding the first coming of Christ, but what of the second? What of the fateful hour, known to God alone, when Christ returns to judge the world? When will God's clock strike again to announce 'the Day of the Lord'? What time is set for his coming in majesty and great glory? The Advent season makes us expectant of Christmas—but what has happened to our expectancy of the second Advent? Advent hymns are heartily sung—'Lo! He comes with clouds descending . . . Christ appears on earth to reign'—but do we believe them? Are we eagerly anticipating Christ's return? Nothing is more certain:

Christ on oath, affirmed it (Matthew 26.64).
The angels of God confirmed it (Acts 1.11).
The apostles preached it (2 Thessalonians 2).
The Church believed it.

It was this deeply held conviction of Christ's return that made the early Church so zealous to serve. The thought of their returning Lord, to whom they would have each to give account, made them faithful in work and witness. The parable of the returning Bride-

4

groom kept the flame of faith and hope alive. Diligent reading of the Scriptures made them watch for the signs of his return. All history they realized was *his*-story. They looked eagerly for the final chapter, the denouement, when Christ would return in power and great glory. They believed God was working his purpose out, as year succeeds to year, and thus life took on a serious purpose and a dynamic meaning. Christians in every generation have continued to believe that God is working his purpose out as time ticks on towards God's appointed hour.

Dare we then, in our own day and generation, push the truth of Christ's coming to the back of our minds? Can we continue to live if Christ were not already on his way? Present world-conditions tell us that time is short. The Bible tells us to beware, and Jesus himself warns us: 'Watch therefore, for ye know neither the day nor the hour wherein the Son of man cometh' (Matthew 25.13). The final word of the risen and ascended Lord promises: 'Surely I come quickly. Amen.' To which faith replies: 'Even so, come, Lord Jesus' (Revelation 22.20).

BIBLE SUNDAY
The Scrolls of Salvation

From a child thou hast known the holy scriptures, which are able to make thee wise unto salvation through faith which is in Christ Jesus.

2 TIMOTHY 3.15

KNOWN FROM CHILDHOOD

That's true! I *have* been acquainted with the Scriptures ever since as a child I was given by my Sunday school teacher little texts of scripture printed on a card with a picture which I took home to show to mother. I don't claim actually to have 'known' the Scriptures, but I was certainly acquainted with them. One card of which I was particularly proud had words painted with phosphorus which glowed in the darkness – 'God is Love'. Since those childhood days, I have acquired about a dozen Bibles, some in Latin, some in Hebrew, some in Greek, together with a number of modern translations into English. They stand in a honoured row on the top shelf of my bookcase. But the Bible I bought last was, oddly enough, the King James Version with which I first began. It lies before me now. It is a handsome publication, well bound, with a gold-lined cover, and containing the majestic and moving language of English at its best. It commended itself to me by being in big print! As I hold it now, and turn its pages, I marvel at the multitude of cross-references, and up-to-date maps.

AT WHAT COST?

Even more I marvel at the heroic deeds of history which have finally brought it into my hands. I think of Moses with his engraved tablets of stone. I think of the persecuted prophets and their scribes. I think of the evangelists and the apostles braving the edicts of a mad Emperor and the fearsome power of Rome. I think of cold monastic cells where the intricate work of copying was painfully carried on year after year. I think of the dedicated succession of scholars and translators, and of their labour of love down the centuries. I think of the Dead Sea Scrolls preserved thousands of years in hidden caves. I think of the papyrus and vellum scrolls, and the yellowing pages of Scriptures which have come down to us from the persecuted Church, stained with the tears and blood of the martyrs. To pass on this Bible which I now hold in my hands, men have gone to the torture-chamber and the stake of burning; and I am reminded of the brave words of Bishop Latimer he called to his fellow-sufferer, as the flaming torch was put to the faggots of their martyrdom:

> Be of good comfort, Master Ridley, and play the man. We shall this day light such a candle by God's grace in England, as (I trust) shall never be put out.

And what shall be said of the Bible Societies with their tremendous task of translating and printing of the Scriptures in over a thousand different languages; and the taking of them by missionaries and colporteurs to people all over the world? When I pick up this Bible I have a vision of the heroes, crossing mountains, fording treacherous rivers, and enduring incredible hardships and dangers, in their determination to bring the Word of God to those who sit in darkness and in the shadow of death. I am reminded of the epic of Ron Russell, the lone yachtsman, who abandoned his voyage around the world in order to deliver Bibles to the million and a half people in the sixteen islands spread across the vastness of the Pacific Ocean. He was provided with portions of the Scriptures in their 265 different languages and dialects!

BEYOND PRICE

What price shall be put on Bibles provided at such cost? Collectors of rare books find the most ancient copies of the Bible far beyond their financial reach. It took government funds to buy the fourth-century Codex Sinaiticus at a cost of £100,000, after it narrowly escaped being thrown into the boiler fire of the monastery where it was discovered. Some priceless copies are coveted more than the Kohinoor diamond of England's Crown. Yet one society (The Scripture Gift Mission) actually gives gospels away!

The policy of the British and Foreign Bible Society is to supply Scriptures to every man at the price he can afford. The value of the Scriptures and the precious truths of the Bible cannot be calculated in cash. There is profit in them, we know, but it is a profit far above the values of the Stock Exchange. 'All scripture is given by inspiration of God, and is profitable', said St Paul (2 Timothy 3.16); but the profit he meant was spiritual, not material. It is – 'to make thee wise unto salvation'. 'For what shall it profit a man if he gain the whole world, and lose his own soul?' said Jesus (Matthew 16.26). When I was very young my godly old aunt gave me a label to stick in the front of my Bible. It reads:

> Its doctrines are holy . . . read it to be wise, believe it to be safe, and practise it to be holy. It contains light to direct you, food to support you, and comfort to cheer you. It is the traveller's map, the pilgrim's staff, the pilot's compass, and the soldier's sword.

You may think this high-flown language, but she lived by it, and so do I! Over many years, I have yet to find those words untrue.

A MODERN MARVEL

Everyone ought to possess a Bible. By the marvels of modern publishing the ancient scripts, once contained in many unwieldy scrolls, are now available in convenient paperbacks, or library editions. The days of forbidding black Bibles with narrow columns and hard-to-read print are gone for ever. Although many will still love the majestic prose of the King James Version (AD 1611) others will be glad to see the many modern translations in the language of today. They are attractive, clearly printed, and cheap to buy. Although a book with a long history, yet the Bible is also a very modern book. It is as up-to-date as tomorrow's newspaper! It is now computerized and recorded on cassettes and compact discs. It is still one of the world's best sellers, and the printing presses continue to pour out millions of copies. It is produced in braille for the blind, and in books that talk to the handicapped. Copies of the Gideon Bibles are to be found in most hotel rooms all over the world. The admirable layout of the contents makes them clear to any who seek in them the answer to their spiritual problems.

DIGGING OUT ITS TREASURE

It is no use possessing a valuable book, however, if it is left unread. So let us look inside the covers, and dig out the hidden treasures. The first thing we discover is that the Bible is not one book but many—a whole library, 66 books in all. Turning the pages we come across books of history, books of poetry, law-books, prophetic books, ancient chronicles, songbooks, love stories, and a collection of wise proverbs. Then, of course, we have the four gospels, the Acts of the Apostles, and the letters of St Paul and other apostles. Finally, we reach the book of Revelation, which makes a promise of blessing to everyone who reads it.

So we are presented with a collection of sacred writings, covering a period of over sixteen hundred years, written by many different authors; who lived in different ages, sometimes separated by centuries from the previous penmen. Moreover, they wrote in several different languages, and from a cultural background far different from our own. Yet, they are intended for everyman, of every age, of every nation, and of every rank from kings and cabinet ministers downwards. Prime Minister Gladstone, in a time of national crisis, was heard to say 'I must point to the old, old, story, told in an old, old, book . . . the greatest and best gift ever given to mankind.'

How then shall we begin to read and understand it? I have three simple suggestions to offer—the three R's of Bible-reading.

1. Read it reverently
This is a holy book. It is about God, and inspired by God. Although written by human hands the inspiration was divine. 'For the prophecy came not in old time by the will of man: but holy men of God spake as they were moved by the Holy Ghost' (2 Peter 1.21). This holy book, therefore, needs to be approached reverently, and read with humility. There must be a readiness to submit to its truths. Intellectual arrogance, or a stubborn will, will inevitably block its message to the soul. We might well begin with the ancient prayer that he who inspired it would now interpret it, and make it clear to our understanding.

'Open thou mine eyes, that I may behold wondrous things out of thy law' (Psalm 119.18).

2. Read it regularly
Do not read it sporadically, haphazardly chancing on this passage of Scripture or that. Have a plan, a system of daily readings which

will chart a course through the Scriptures without confusion. No
intelligent person enters the public library and idly picks out books
to read without reference to the section-headings. He doesn't con-
fuse poetry with prose, fact with fiction, nor children's stories with
manuals of technology. The Bible Reading Fellowship and the
Scripture Union provide clear straightforward guidance for reading
the Bible in a systematic way. It is a good idea to read a portion
of Scripture every day. The late King of England read a chapter
a day.

3. *Read it right through*
By this I don't mean 'plough through it' from Genesis to Revelation;
although even that would be preferable to picking out passages here
and there at random, like a hen pecking corn. No! I mean have the
aim of knowing the whole Bible, achieving it in the most sensible
way by following one or other of the above mentioned reading-
schemes. They will give you an aerial view of the territory to be
explored and, as you move through the Bible in this manner, you
will find that one passage will throw light upon another. Despite
all the differences, you will discover their divine unity, for behind
the many writers there is the one God who inspired them.

4. Finally, remember that *Christ is the key to the Scriptures*
He is the grand Subject of them all. When the risen Christ walked
with the disciples on the road to Emmaus he gave them a Bible
lesson that literally glowed: '. . . beginning at Moses and all the
prophets, he expounded unto them in all the scriptures the things
concerning himself' (Luke 24.27). He opened their eyes to understand what the Scriptures were saying, unlocked the mystery of
the ages, and warmed their hearts with the glad realization of who
he really is—the Saviour of the world!

THE FEAST OF DEDICATION
When Winter Comes

It was at Jerusalem the feast of the dedication, and it was winter.
And Jesus walked in the temple in Solomon's porch.

JOHN 10.22, 23

DARK DAYS

I'm glad Jesus went to the Temple in winter, for it brought realism into religion. Many people have a sentimental picture of Jerusalem bathed in the golden sunshine of summer: but note that Christ worshipped there in the Temple in winter. Jerusalem in December can be very wet and cold. A snow-fall of sixteen inches in one night has been recorded, when the main road from the capital to the coast was blocked by drifts. Just how bad the conditions were when Jesus walked in to worship that winter we do not know, but we do know that it was at the winter solstice; it was when the sun was at its furthest, and the day at its darkest. Jesus walked into the Temple when the temperature was at its lowest. How many others attended on that dismal day we are not told, but we know that Jesus was there, and it made all the difference. What a difference it would make to church-attendance in winter, if people were sure they would find Jesus there! It is one thing to sing of 'Jerusalem the Golden' when the summer suns are glowing; but quite another when the temperature drops, and the flame of faith burns low.

THE FESTIVAL OF LIGHT

In an attempt to dispel the darkness of doubt in religion, the Jews organized a great festival of light, known as The Feast of the Dedication. It commemorated the religious victory over the darkness of heathenism in the reign of Antiochus Epiphanes (*c.* 150 BC). He had infuriated the Jews by burning their Scriptures, and defiling their Temple; installing an image of Jupiter, and sacrificing swine upon the holy altar of God. Prior to the Macccabean revolt,

11

it was, indeed, the dark winter of religion. After the successful revolt, however, the Temple was ceremonially cleansed, and re-dedicated; and it was decided to commemorate this glad event each year in December by holding a Festival of Light. It began with the ceremonial lighting of the golden candelabra in the Temple, and continued during the next eight days with the shining of oil-lamps in the windows of every Jewish home in Jerusalem. Thousands of lights shone across the city. It was this festival that Jesus decided to attend on that dark December day. 'And it was at Jerusalem the feast of the dedication, and it was winter. And Jesus walked in the temple in Solomon's porch' (John 10.22, 23). It was at the dramatic moment of the lighting of the golden candlesticks that Jesus, the Light of the world, suddenly came to his Temple. He came to people who sat in darkness and the shadow of death. To those whose spirits were low he came. And he made his entrance through Solomon's porch! For the occasion the porch of Solomon had been polished and decorated. Bright light fell on burnished shields and other symbols of that splendid reign; but, at the very moment that men's minds were on past glories and a dead king, the Living Lord came in! 'Behold, a greater than Solomon is here!' (Matthew 12.42). The King of Glory came suddenly into his Temple.

THE LIGHT OF CHRIST

At the darkest hour he came. At the winter solstice of the soul he came. On the darkest of days 'The Sun of Righteousness had arisen with healing in His wings'. Men remembered the tremendous day in history when the building of Solomon's Temple was finished and dedicated with great splendour to the glory of God. At that time, a mysterious radiance filled the house of the Lord. They called it the Shekinah—'The Glory', the light which betokened the presence of God in the portable temple used by Moses in the desert-journeying. Now it had appeared again! This was the Glory of which men spoke with bated breath. It was the Glory the shepherds saw in the highest, when the angels sang of the Saviour's birth. Now, as Jesus walked in Solomon's porch, it shone again! His entrance brought in the light of God's presence. The Glory, long departed from the temple, appeared again. The Light of the world had come.

Over some 'sacred places', once radiant with the presence of God, now hangs the dreaded word—'Ichabod!' ('The Glory of God has departed': see 1 Samuel 4.21). God has gone, and with the withdrawal of God has come the fading of the heavenly glow. Darkness has descended upon the so-called house of God. The form of words and the outward rituals may remain, but the heavenly light has faded. Outwardly the church remains a consecrated building, but it seems but an empty shell. God has gone, and so has the congregation! A few loyal folk may remain, but their faith tends to grow cold and their prayers become weak. An awful emptiness has chilled the soul. God is no longer experienced in such a place. There is no need to write 'Ichabod': it is sensed as soon as one enters. Elderly parishioners struggle on with memories of the former state, but it has become the place of shadows.

WHEN CHRIST COMES IN

What a difference it makes when Christ enters and is welcomed, trusted, and obeyed! Then God's glory returns. The place is transformed. The pulpit throbs again as Christ is preached in all his saving power. The lectern again sets forth the living Word. The altar turns into the sacred table of the Lord where souls are fed, and the empty pews fill again with people seeking to pray. Oh what a glorious difference it makes to worship when Christ enters the door!

As it was then, so will it be now, for the same Jesus who walked into the Temple on that cold winter's day, so long ago, still longs to enter our churches and our hearts, today. He strides down the centuries to bring light and life to our own day and generation. He comes to warm, and light, and cheer. He stands at our heart's door with the lamp of God in his hand, for this is the day of his visitation. This is the day of opportunity. For this is the moment for which, unconsciously, we have been waiting. Whatever our failures and sins in the years that have passed, we have but to ask him to enter our souls, to rejoice in his light and love within. Together with the Apostle we shall be able to say

God, who commanded the light to shine out of darkness, hath shined in our hearts, to give the light of the knowledge of the glory of God in the face of Jesus Christ. (2 Corinthians 4.6)

CHRISTMAS
The Song and the Sign

The shepherds said one to another, Let us now go even unto Bethlehem, and see this thing which is come to pass, which the Lord hath made known unto us.

LUKE 2.15

It was uncomfortable and cold on Christmas Eve, and there was grumbling as the shepherds gathered around their watch-fire. Often, they peered into the darkness, clutching their staves to beat off any attack by prowling wolves. Christmas did not start well for them, but it turned out to be the most wonderful experience of their lives. With amazement they saw the blackness of the night brighten with the radiance of God's glory. They heard heavenly music, and saw a vision of angels; but, best of all, they saw the Christ Child. 'And the shepherds returned, glorifying and praising God for all the things they had heard and seen' (Luke 2.20). At this season may we share the joy of the shepherds and, after the midnight service of Holy Communion, return home praising God for all the things we have heard and seen.

THE CIRCUMSTANCE OF CHRISTMAS

In actual fact, however, not all people will enjoy Christmas this year. Circumstances alter cases. The homeless and the hungry will find it hard to rejoice. People in lands of deprivation and starvation will hardly be able to return home 'glorifying and praising God' — especially if they have no home to go back to! The unemployed, and those unable to meet their mortgage repayments, will find it difficult to celebrate, and what Christmas cheer will there be for people trying to sleep in cardboard boxes? Can folk in such cruel circumstances be happy at Christmas?

Philosophers, from their warm study and the ease of their arm-chair, inform us that while 'happiness' depends on what 'happens',

14

'contentment' is independent of outward circumstance! Meditating monks, and mystics, draw a distinction between 'happiness' and 'joy'. Christian joy, they say, comes not from outward happenings and comfortable circumstances, but from the indwelling Christ. Furthermore, this experience is not confined to mystics, but may gladden ordinary believers, despite adverse circumstances.

I remember one particularly uncomfortable Christmas, spent on a rat-infested ship, anchored in the grey waters of Loch Foyle. Fifteen miles from the nearest friendly port, blacked-out against the threat of enemy aircraft, on watch in the bitterly cold north wind; conditions were not conducive to celebration! (Ironically, we could see through binoculars the bright lights of a neutral town in Eire where they celebrated without war's restrictions.) Christmas dinner was cooked in a makeshift kitchen on the open deck, where it was swiftly chilled before we could eat it. With our families at home in danger of bombing, we felt our circumstance was hardly one of Christmas cheer. Nevertheless, the day became increasing joyous as the message of Christmas came through. Like the shepherds of old, we took it in turns to keep watch and, like them, wrapped warmly against the bitter cold. So, once more, like the shepherds, we shared the joy of Christmas Day.

THE CELEBRATION OF CHRISTMAS

How then, and why, should we celebrate that Christmas of long ago? For what reason should we festoon our streets and homes with fairy lights, hold parties, and arrange family gatherings? Why take all the trouble to purchase presents, cook turkeys, and decorate the traditional tree? Why on Christmas Eve do we drag ourselves away from the home fires, and trudge through snow and rain to cold churches, at midnight? What is there to celebrate? Surely it is much more than ancient custom that brings out many, and gladdens the night. Why has the Christmas story captured so many hearts? And why has the ancient tale of a child born in poverty and laid in a manger continued to stir the modern mind? What is it that causes so many at Christmas to give to the hungry, the homeless, and the outcasts of society? Appeals for charity at Christmas rarely fall on deaf ears. Is it because the Holy Family found no room in the inn? Or is it that the 'Love which came down at Christmas' has now found lodging in our hearts?

15

THE CORE OF CHRISTMAS

There is much more to Christmas, however, than a heart-stirring story, and a time-honoured custom. Wherein lies the deeper meaning and the true substance of the story; and how shall we get beyond the tinsel, and the trimmings, and the Christmas tree? When Christmas is over, what shall we 'keep and ponder in our mind'? Shall it be the mystery of the Word made flesh, or 'God's wondrous love in saving lost mankind'? Whilst many like to think of Christmas in the human terms of a man, and a maid, and a Babe laid in a manger; they sense there is much more, and ask what is Christmas really about? We can sum it up under three headings.

1. *It is about a Song*
It is about the song of the angels, the heavenly song of God, and of peace among men of good will. It was the song that dispelled the fear and darkness of man's night. So often in the blackout when the bombs were falling on London, folk in underground shelters joined in this prayer: 'Lighten our darkness, we beseech Thee, O Lord; and by thy great mercy defend us from all perils and dangers of this night.' Did the shepherds pray that night? If so, their prayer was marvellously answered:

> And the glory of the Lord shone round about them . . . And the angel said unto them, Fear not: . . . And suddenly there was with the angel a multitude of the heavenly host praising God, and saying, Glory to God in the highest, and on earth peace, good will toward men. (Luke 2.9–14)

That was a song to beat all songs, and sung by a choir to beat all choirs—the song of the heavenly host. The shepherds were enchanted. It was the first Christmas carol!

2. *It was about a Saviour*
It was a song about a Saviour born to deliver men from fear, to save those who sat in darkness and in the shadow of death. It was about one called Jesus 'for he shall save his people from their sins' (Matthew 1.21). It was about the great Liberator, who 'breaks the bonds of cancelled sin, and sets the prisoner free'. 'For unto you is born this day a Saviour, which is Christ the Lord.'

3. *Thirdly, Christmas was not only about a song, and a Saviour, but also about a Sign*

'And this shall be a sign unto you; Ye shall find the babe wrapped in swaddling clothes, lying in a manger.' Other babies may have been born in Bethlehem that night, but only one was born in a stable. Only he, the Divine Son of God, and Prince of Peace had to make do with a manger for his bed! Only *he* was wrapped in rags, bound in swaddling clothes and laid in a manger. It was for a *sign*, the sign of his poverty and identification with the poor and lowly. To bind the limbs of a newborn babe in an effort to keep them straight was a common Eastern custom; but the shepherds were given to see the swaddling clothes as a sign, a sign of the Saviour who consented to be bound for us. Oh, the love and humility of the strong Son of God, who consented to be a baby, to be *bound* with human limitations, to live a life of poverty, to share our sorrows, and spare no sacrifice to save sinners!

He, the Heavenly Prince, came down to share our lot. He laid aside his riches, and stripped himself of everything, but love. He made himself of no reputation, and for our sakes took upon himself the form of a servant. As man, he humbled himself, and became obedient unto death, even the death of the cross! (Philippians 2.6). Marvelling at this amazing grace, St Paul exclaimed:

> For you know the grace of our Lord Jesus Christ that, though he was rich, yet for your sake he became poor, that ye through his poverty might be rich. (2 Corinthians 8.9)

'They *bound* him . . .' Significantly, in the account of the crucifixion, the evangelist says the soldiers 'set him at nought', they stripped, and bound him. As in the cradle, so on the cross! He died in like manner as he was born—of no reputation, naked, bound—and all for love of us men, and for our salvation. Alleluia! What a Saviour!

THE NEW YEAR
Whither Bound?

If I have found grace in thy sight, show me now thy way.

EXODUS 33.13

PLOTTING OUR POSITION

As the old-time sailing ships crossed by each other on the vast oceans of the world, they used to shout 'Whither bound?' It's a good question to ask ourselves at the start of a New Year. 'Whither bound?' Where are we heading? And what course do we need to follow? No one wants to be an aimless drifter through this life, and to miss his true destination in the next. As all navigators know, it is essential to log the miles passed, to fix the present position, and then to plot the future course. So too must we on the journey of life. But what if we are in uncharted seas, if the future is all unknown, and we do not know the way?

As we enter the New Year with the future all unknown, we must first look over the past with the misfortunes and mistakes which have thrown us off course. We need to check our present position in the sight of God, for there are deviations to be corrected, relationships to be repaired, and sins for which to repent. Forgiveness needs to be found, and restitution made before we can turn over the stained page of the past. But the year ahead is unsullied. The chart of the future lies clean and waiting to be plotted – *if only we knew the way*!

DECIDING OUR COURSE

So here is a prayer for guidance. '*If I have found grace in thy sight, show me now thy way*' (Exodus 33.13). It was the prayer of Moses for himself and the people of God, as they wandered along an unknown way across the bewildering wilderness. They had fled from Egypt, crossed the Red Sea, and started their journey with high hopes. Behind them were the days of slavery, ahead of them

18

the promise of a land flowing with milk and honey; but so far they had found only sand and stones, and a landscape of rugged rocks. Having lost sense of direction they began to grumble against the leadership and turned aside from the worship of God to idols of gold—as do many today. When Moses came down from the Mount of God, drawn by the din of drums and dancing, he saw the golden calf and the abandonment to sin. In righteous anger he dashed to the ground the broken laws of God, and left the stone inscriptions there to shame the sinners. Then Moses returned unto the Lord, and said

> Oh, this people have sinned a great sin, and have made them gods of gold. Yet now, if thou wilt forgive their sin—; and if not, blot me, I pray thee, out of thy book which thou hast written. And the Lord said unto Moses, Whosoever hath sinned against me, him will I blot out of my book . . . in the day when I visit, I will visit their sin upon them. (Exodus 32.31-34)

Here is a word of God not only for the people of a past age, but also for the people of our time, for the 'permissive society', and for those who endorse the so-called 'new morality' of our modern age. *There is no new morality, only the old immorality; and the terrible consequences which remain the same, if there is no repentance.*

NEEDING OUR GUIDE

Many years ago, I was lost in an African forest. Its paths were many, narrow, and intersected; and the tall trees hid every landmark. Darkness was about to fall, and I was feeling desperate. I am sure I must have uttered an urgent prayer, for the answer came in the form of an African carrying a fish-spear. Although he spoke no English he seemed to understand my need to be shown the way, for without a word he pointed to himself, turned on his heel, and beckoned me to follow. At a rapid pace, with turn after twisting turn, he led me through the entangled undergrowth, until I was in sight of safety. Pointing to himself, he seemed to say 'I am the way'. In answer to my prayer, God gave me not a guidebook but a guide. So it was when Thomas asked 'Lord . . . how can we know the way?' that Jesus replied 'I am the way, the truth, and the life', or as it may be translated, 'I am the true and living way' (John 14.6). On Christmas day 1939 King George VI made the customary broadcast to the nation. World war had darkened the streets, and the windows of every house were blacked-out as a precaution against enemy bombing. The king's message was one of courage and faith, and was relevant to the fears many felt. But it was his concluding quotation of this poem which sticks in my memory:

And I said to the man who stood at the gate of the year
Give me a light that I may tread safely into the unknown.
And he replied – Go out into the darkness,
and put your hand into the hand of God.
That shall be to you better than a light,
and safer than a known way. (Minnie Louise Haskins)

HOW GOD GUIDES

How then does God guide?

(a) *By his answers to our prayers*
Be assured of this, that God gives guidance to those who seek it from him. Moses, charged to lead the people through the trackless desert, bowed before God and prayed:

Thou sayest unto me, Bring up this people: and thou hast not let me know whom thou wilt send with me . . . Now therefore, I pray thee, if I have found grace in thy sight, shew me now thy way. (Exodus 33.12–13)

In times of perplexity prayer is our first resource. Put your problem before the Lord. When David Livingstone ventured into the Dark Continent, he didn't blunder on blindly. Daily he used his compass and sextant, and took his bearings, but first, each day he knelt in prayer. In his journal he wrote 'Thank God for his mercies so far . . . I commit my way to Thee. I trust that thou wilt direct my steps.'

(b) *By the assurance of his presence*
When Moses prayed 'whom wilt thou send with me?' Who will be my guide? God answered: 'My presence shall go with thee, and I will give thee rest.' I take that word 'rest' to mean rest of mind, reassurance when in doubt, the peace of God which passeth all understanding. In every situation, in every danger, Moses was to know that God himself was with him. As supernatural tokens of that presence Moses was given the guiding cloud by day, and the pillar of fire by night. When the people thirsted, the rock was riven and water given; when they hungered, manna was found on the ground

20

and food fell from the sky. But today we do not have such signs. How shall we have the assurance of his presence? It is true that in this era, and on our Christian pilgrimage, we walk by faith and not by sight. But God's promise still applies, and is repeated to us in the words of Jesus, 'Lo, I am with you always' (Matthew 28.20). The tokens of God's grace and abiding presence, though different, are still given. They are given in the answers to our prayers. They are given in the bread and the wine of Holy Communion. They are given in the witness of God's Spirit within. They are found in the reading of God's word; and they are experienced in the rest God gives to our souls. 'For he hath said, I will never leave thee, nor forsake thee' (Hebrews 13.5).

(c) *By the sending of his Son*
Scripture says:

> God, who at sundry times and in divers manners spake in time past unto the fathers by the prophets, hath in these last days spoken unto us by his Son. (Hebrews 1.1)

Of all the signs and symbols given by God to guide the sons of men, the greatest is seen in the gift of God's own Son. Through him God speaks most clearly. He was the Divine Word made flesh, who came to dwell among us. He came as the Divine Light to dispel the darkness, and to lead us in his way. Of those who walked with him, John exclaimed with awe 'And we beheld his glory, the glory as of the only begotten of the Father, full of grace and truth' (John 1.14). The glory of God was seen at his birth, when the angels sang. It was manifested at his first miracle in Cana of Galilee. It shone in his teaching, and healing, and leading men to God. It was demonstrated in his character when he showed men how to live. Above all it was revealed in the cross of glory when he taught us how to ie. In Jesus, God gave us not a guidebook, but a Guide, to lead us in his way, a Divine Shepherd who calls us to follow. He is the true way, and the living example we need to follow closely throughout this New Year.

> Almighty God, who hast given thine only Son to be unto us both a sacrifice for sin, and also an example of godly life: Give us grace that we may always most thankfully receive that his inestimable benefit, and also daily endeavour ourselves *to follow the blessed steps of his most holy life*; through the same Jesus Christ our Lord. Amen. (Book of Common Prayer)

21

THE EPIPHANY
The Quest of the Wise

*Now when Jesus was born in Bethlehem of Judaea in the days of
Herod the king, behold, there came wise men from the east to
Jerusalem . . .*

MATTHEW 2.1

THE MEN OF MYSTERY

The wise men from the East were, and remain, men of mystery.
In wartime from an airfield on the southern edge of the Sahara
Desert, we overlooked the ancient trade route used by camel trains
to bring goods to the walled city of Kano. From time to time, we
saw a cloud of dust in the distance, out of which would appear Arab
traders, escorted by fierce-looking horsemen, armed, veiled, and
unspeaking. Trading done, they would disappear into the distance
as mysteriously as they had come. We learned neither their names,
nor country of origin. We thought they might have come from
distant Timbuktu! Like the Magi in Matthew's gospel, the veiled
Tuareg, lords of the desert, were men of mystery. 'If captured,
give only your number, rank, and name!' we were ordered. But,
regarding the Magi, not even these meagre details are given. The
gospel has drawn the veil of anonymity over the wise men from the
east, who came to Jesus at his Epiphany.

As with all mysteries, speculation has been rife, and legend has
tried to fill in what the evangelist left out. Some supposed, because
of the three mystic gifts, that the number of men was three. Others
thought the Magi were kings because of the prophetic words
'Gentiles shall come to thy light, and *kings* to the brightness of thy
rising' (Isaiah 60.3).

The venerable Bede, with pious imagination, supplied their
names, nationality, and even a note on their personal appearance!
Melchior, he said, was an old man with a long white beard; Caspar,
a ruddy and beardless youth; whereas Balthasar was swarthy and
in the prime of life. The first was a descendant of Shem, the second
of Ham, and the third of Japheth—thus representing the three main

racial roots of mankind. If Bede were right, then the searchers might represent anyone in search of truth, whatever his age, rank, or race.

Useful though these speculations proved to the poets and hymn-writers, and the artists who have tried to paint the Epiphany scene; yet honesty forbids us to take them as more than imaginary embellishments of the gospel. Like their 'solemn gifts of mystic meaning' the Magi remain a mystery.

THE STAR OF REVELATION

If the star led to Christ, then we can take it to be the star of revelation, well placed at the beginning of the gospels, which reveal Christ as the Way, the Truth, and the Life. If the wise men were students of the stars, and worshippers of light; then they may represent all who seek to find in Christ the True Light. If these were kings from foreign nations who knelt to the infant Christ, did they see in him the Light of the world? The star of Epiphany recalls other scriptural references to stars. One ancient prophecy of the Messiah says 'There shall come a Star out of Jacob' (Numbers 24.17).

The Book of Revelation (22.16) calls Christ 'The Morning Star'. In the epistles, Jesus is referred to as 'a light shining in a dark place, until the day dawn, and the day star arise in your hearts' (2 Peter 1.19).

THE SPIRIT OF THEIR SEARCH

The motivation of the Magi, and the diligent spirit in which they persisted in their long search for truth, still inspire those who wish to make the journey of faith. Even at this distance of time, the Magi challenge heart, and mind, and will. The truth of God is not found easily; it demands an open mind, a determined will, and a generous heart. The star of revelation was not shown to the cynical but to men of faith, to the wise, the sincere, and those willing to follow wherever God might lead. The Magi, however primitive their religion, had *faith to follow*, and they loved the light. The star they regarded as God-given guidance, which they were ready to follow. Josephus, a historian of that time, recorded the intense expectancy prevailing throughout the entire East, that a powerful leader would come from Judaea to deliver the oppressed millions. A light would arise for those who sat in darkness and in the shadow of death. It was this expectancy of faith that made the Magi into pilgrims.

These were no armchair scholars debating religion, but explorers ready to face hardship. With admirable courage and resolve they determined to follow the light at whatever cost, and to continue wherever it led, and however long it took to find. Their quest proved to be neither short nor easy. Sometimes we sing 'as with joyful steps they sped, Saviour to thy lowly bed'; but often their steps must have been painfully slow. Their long journey over the mountains and across the deserts must have seemed endless. It took not weeks, but months, and possibly years. If Herod, having questioned the Magi what time the star appeared, then slew all children in Bethlehem 'from two years old and under' (Matthew 2.16)—might that indicate how long their journey took? Often they must have felt like abandoning the search as time and hardship tested their resolve; but they had what the saints have called *the grace of continuance*. We cannot but admire their persistence. God rewards those who keep right on to the end.

We of the West can hardly credit men marching after a star. We do have not the Eastern mind, nor their belief in astrology. These men, however, believed that the destiny of mankind was written in the stars; and the sight of a new bright star would have made a deep impression. Here were men who had spent their lives studying the stars, and who pioneered astral navigation across the trackless desert sands. They were men of great vigour and also of great *intellectual integrity*. They would go to any lengths to find a fact. Before we get too superior about their superstitions, let us remember that modern mathematics and astronomy owes much to the ancient East.

Finally, remember not only their courageous intellect but also their *humility and reverence*. They came to *kneel*! 'We have seen his star in the east and are come to worship him' (Matthew 2.2). The greater the scholar, the greater his humility and reverence for truth. Kepler, the greatest astronomer of the seventeenth century, noted a bright new star, following the conjunction of the two largest planets in December 1603, a brightness which gradually faded after one year. Knowing the gospel story and what a deep impression such a star would have made upon the Magi, he calculated backwards from his day to theirs, and estimated that a similar star might well have been seen at the time of the Magi.

24

THE INSPIRATION THEY PROVIDE

The Magi might have been disciples of Zoroaster the fire-worshipper, but whatever the incompleteness of that religion, it kindled in them love of light and zeal to discover the truth. Zealously following what little light they had, even though but a glimmer in the midnight sky, it finally brought them to Christ; in whom all wisdom and truth is found. They felt they had found in him the Light of the world; and so, having presented their gifts, they knelt humbly in wonder, praise, and adoration.

The symbolic meaning of their mystic gifts remains as great a mystery as the men themselves. Christian devotion looks upon the gold as a tribute to Christ's kingship, frankincense as an offering to his divinity, and myrrh as a foretoken of his saving death. But what lies beyond question is the inspiration the Magi have given to the worship of the Church down the centuries. In liturgy, poetry, music, and works of art, the Epiphany scene has been set forth in matchless beauty; and the Wise Men have shown in what spirit we are to take up our own personal pilgrimage. By their humility, generosity, and willing obedience they encourage us all to worship in spirit and in truth. How better could this be expressed than in the lovely hymn?

> O worship the Lord in the beauty of holiness!
> Bow down before Him, his glory proclaim;
> With gold of obedience, and incense of lowliness,
> Kneel and adore Him: The Lord is his name.
>
> (J. S. B. Monsell)

THE CONVERSION OF ST PAUL (January 25)
On Keeping Faith

The time of my departure is at hand. I have fought a good fight, I have finished my course, I have kept the faith.

2 TIMOTHY 4.6, 7

This was St Paul's summary and assessment of his life in a farewell letter to Timothy, written shortly before his execution. He urged him to continue the good fight of faith and to endure hardship as a good soldier of Jesus Christ. Like a relay runner, he then handed on the torch of truth, which he had kept at the cost of his life. Looking over that life, it becomes clear that St Paul regarded his conversion to Christ on the Damascus road as the most important event of his whole existence. He declared 'for me to live is Christ'. His conversion changed him from Saul the persecutor to Paul the Apostle. He became Christ's ambassador to the nations of the world. The universal Church commemorates the day of St Paul's conversion, for without it and his passion to reach 'the regions beyond', Christianity might have been long delayed in its evangelization of the nations. The influence of his life and letters on the worldwide Church has been immense.

CARICATURED

Yet, like many another great person, he has been at times grossly misrepresented and cruelly cartooned. The 'Spitting Image' of TV notoriety has been tried in previous centuries. A hundred years ago, Ernest Renan cynically described St Paul as 'the ugly little Jew'; and even in the second century a semi-historical novel portrayed Paul as 'That short, bald, bow-legged man, with grizzled beard, greyish eyes, knitted eyebrows, long nose, and stooping shoulders; looking now like a man, and now like an angel!' (the *Acts of Paul and Thecla*). But, in leaving fiction for fact, we have to confess that we do not really *know* what St Paul looked like. All that we know that bears on his physical appearance is that he suffered from the strain of bad eyesight, that his back bore the scars of repeated flogging (as did his Master's), and what he called his constant 'thorn in the flesh' (see 2 Corinthians 12.7) must have left lines of suffering on his brow. Also, he must have been physically tough to endure all the hardships he had to bear. We know more about his mental make-up than his physical appearance. He had a brilliant and well-educated mind. As the son and grandson of a Pharisee, he was determined to become a Pharisee. He left the university town of Tarsus, where he had been brought up, in order to study in the Jerusalem School of Rabbinics, under the famous scholar Gamaliel. There in study and in his zeal to follow the religious traditions of his race, he swiftly came to the fore. Although a Hebrew of the Hebrews, yet he was also acquainted with the Greek culture he had learnt in Tarsus. He spoke the language fluently and quoted from the Greek poets. The main trade roots ran through his home town, which thus had a cosmopolitan flavour, and further stretched his mental horizons. Yet, that potentially great mind was torn between high religious aspiration and low moral performance. Had not Christ arrested him on his mission of persecution, the road to Damascus would have been the road to damnation.

CONVERTED

The difficulty in trying to describe Paul is double vision. We see not one man, but two! On the one hand we see Saul of Tarsus, the harsh persecutor of the Church, and on the other hand St Paul, the loving Apostle of Christ. The transformation was so swift and total that neither Jew nor Christian could believe the evidence of their own eyes. Nothing less than a miracle could transform a man so dramatically; yet miracle it was, the miracle of conversion! There was a radical change—total, utter, and final! On his way to Damascus a blinding light, brighter than the sun at noon, threw Saul down to the ground, and brought his cruel mission to a sudden stop. It set his life on an opposite course; for as he lay trembling on the ground, he heard a voice from heaven:

Saul, Saul, why persecutest thou Me? . . . I am Jesus whom thou persecutest. And he, trembling and astonished said, Lord what wilt thou have me to do? and the Lord said unto him, Arise, and go into the city, and it shall be told thee what thou must do. (See Acts 9)

Those who journeyed with him saw only the brilliant flash of light, but Saul saw the Light of the World. He was convinced he had seen Jesus Christ, risen, ascended, and glorified. His conviction was absolute and unswerving. Others could think what they wished: but he knew. Like the man in the gospels, he could say with the utmost certainty 'one thing I know, that whereas I was blind, now I see' (John 10.25). He knew that God had laid hold on him, stopped him in his tracks, spoken with the voice of Christ, and finally flooded his dark soul with heavenly light. He felt like a man born anew, a new creature, a new creation! It was like the Genesis story of creation repeated in his soul. At the word of God darkness gave place to light, deadness to life, and chaos to orderly cosmos. For the God who at the beginning of time said 'Let light shine out of darkness', had now shone into his heart 'to give the light of the knowledge of the glory of God in the face of Jesus Christ' (2 Corinthians 4.6). Before he had encountered Christ his life had been chaotic. He had been bitter, bigoted, and unbelievably cruel. If ever an instance of a soul gone sour were needed, it would be found in Saul before conversion. He was a one-man civil war! He described himself as sold unto sin, possessed, enslaved, and powerless to escape.

> I delight in the law of God after the inward man: But I see another law in my members, warring against the law of my mind, and bringing me into captivity . . . O wretched man that I am! who shall deliver me? (Romans 7.22–24)

His cry of desperation was answered, and is described in the following verses: 'Thank God through Jesus Christ our Lord!' (7.25). 'The Spirit of life in Christ Jesus hath made me *free*!' (8.2). No more does he dwell on his weakness under sin, but on the power of the Spirit. It brought him the blessing of life and peace. The new man in Christ proclaimed 'In all these things we are more than conquerors through him that loved us' (Romans 8.37).

COMMISSIONED

Paul's conversion was followed by his commissioning. Hearing the voice of God brought vocation. The Apostle was commissioned to carry the Gospel of Christ to the Gentile world. His cry of 'Lord, what wilt thou have me to do?' was answered. As he knelt humbly before godly Ananias, the scales fell from his eyes, he received sight forthwith, and he arose, and was baptized; for God had revealed his new mission in life.

> . . . he is a chosen vessel unto me, to bear my name before the Gentiles . . . for I will show him how great things he must suffer for my name's sake. (Acts 9.15–16)

The account of how Paul carried out that commission, as told in the Acts of the Apostles, is an epic of tremendous faith in the face of hardship and suffering. The miles he travelled, the mountains he climbed, the rivers he crossed, the storms he braved, and the mobs he faced, eclipse any adventure tale of fiction.

On a recent tour entitled 'In the Footsteps of Saint Paul', in Greece and Turkey my wife and I were carried in a comfortable coach to many of the places the Apostle had visited *on foot*. We had some tiring walking to do; but only enough to make us marvel at the Apostle who covered many thousands of miles by mule or on foot. In contrast to his ordeal we met no opposition, but he faced hostile mobs, stoning, beating, and imprisonment. 'In weariness and painfulness, in watchings often, in hunger and thirst, in fasting often, in cold and nakedness' (2 Corinthians 11.27). He carried out his commission, as one invested with power and authority by the One to whom all power on earth and in heaven is given. In his letters to the churches he had planted he made a point of announcing his commissioning by Christ: 'I, Paul, called to be an apostle of Jesus Christ through the will of God . . . grace be unto you and peace' (1 Corinthians 1.1, 3).

CROWNED

After his third missionary journey he was arrested, and sent under escort to Rome for trial. There, while awaiting execution, as condemned men do, he looked over his past life. He reviewed all that had happened since the day of his conversion; and summarized life's purpose as a fight to be won, a race to be run, and a faith to be kept. He then wrote his farewell letter to Timothy, to encourage his spiritual son and successor in the faith and service of Christ.

Watch thou in all things, endure afflictions, do the work of an evangelist, make full proof of thy ministry. For I am now ready to be offered, and the time of my departure is at hand. I have fought a good fight, I have finished my course, I have kept the faith: Henceforth there is laid up for me a crown of righteousness, which the Lord, the righteous judge, shall give me at that day: and not to me only, but unto all them also that love his appearing. (2 Timothy 4.5–8)

He pictured the climax and conclusion of the Greek athletic games, the wrestling and relay-racing and the marathon, followed by the presentation of the prizes. Life for the Christian, however, had a more serious purpose, a brighter future, and a better prize then any laurel crown. God would be the judge, and the prize would be no fading wreath of laurel leaves, but an eternal crown of righteousness, given by the Lord on the great day of his appearing.

Paul put the pen down. He was now ready to die, to die in hope. The time of his 'departure' was at hand. Once more he had his eyes on 'the regions beyond'. He used a nautical term for his 'departure'. He was ready to 'cast-off' (*analuseōs*) from the earthly shore, and sail forth on the last and greatest journey of all.

EDUCATION SUNDAY
Clever or Wise?

*Continue thou in the things which thou hast learned and hast been
assured of, knowing of whom thou hast learned them; And that
from a child thou hast known the holy scriptures, which are able
to make thee wise unto salvation through faith which is in
Christ Jesus.*

2 TIMOTHY 3.14–15

THE AIM OF EDUCATION

Today is known as Education Sunday, when the Church puts
children's education at the forefront of her thoughts and prayers.
Both during and after the election, educational theories were subjected to fierce debate, and their claims to success subjected to
intense scrutiny. Adverse comparison has been made with levels of
achievement reached by the children of other nations. According to
the politicians, radical changes of methods must be made, if we as
a nation are to survive in a highly competitive and technological
world. The aim of the good teacher, however, is not to enable his
children merely to 'survive', but to live the good life, and live it to
the full. To be trained for a job, however well paid, is not sufficient.
Good education must prepare children not merely for their working-
days, but for the whole of life including the right use of leisure. It
must teach a child consideration for others, good manners, and right
relationships. Also, if the Scriptures are right in teaching that this
life is but the prelude to the next, then the sense of eternal values
needs to be instilled. *It is more important for a child to become wise
than clever.* Who wants 'a clever devil'? The Scriptures, if well
taught, are able to make one 'wise unto salvation through faith
which is in Christ Jesus'.

PIONEERS OF EDUCATION

The Church can be justly proud of being the pioneer of education in this nation and also, through its missionary societies, of laying the foundation of education in the developing nations. We think of St Augustine founding the first day-school at Canterbury; of Robert Raikes, teaching children to read and write during the early development of the Sunday School movement. The name of Joshua Watson brings to mind the National Society, and the building of Church schools by the thousand. Long before State schools came into being the Church had taken the lead, a fact which has been generously acknowledged by the government of this country. The popularity of Church schools, as shown by the eagerness of parents to have their children entered, bears witness both to the excellence of the dedicated teachers, and also to the value of Christian principles when educating children for the good life. As for other nations and lands abroad, the record of the missionary societies reveals their obedience to the command of Jesus: 'Go ye therefore and teach all nations' (Matthew 28.19).

EDUCATIONAL RESOURCES

What then shall be taught and where are the educational resources for this type of teaching? How shall we make our children wise, kind, and considerate? Where may we find the means to impart the sense of eternal values? Wherein lies the resource material for this 'school for eternity'? St Paul was one of the most highly and widely educated men of his day. From the university city of Tarsus he learned the language and culture of Greece. In Jerusalem he had studied under the great Gamaliel, and was thoroughly trained in Jewish law. From boyhood he had been brought into contact with the cosmopolitan travellers who passed through his home town.

To find a modern parallel scholar of equal intellect, you would need to find a man who could speak Chinese in Peking quoting Confucius and Mencius; who could write closely argued theology in English, and expound it in Oxford; and defend his cause before the Soviet Academy of Sciences in Russian. Just such a man was Paul in his own day! (J. Oswald Sanders)

What source then, does this great scholar recommend for study before all else, in order that a man may be made complete – faithful, wise, and fit for all eternity? In writing to young Timothy, he advised:

> Continue thou in the things which thou hast learned . . . the holy scriptures, which are able to make thee wise unto salvation . . . (2 Timothy 3.14–15)

It is sad to see that the Scripture lesson has disappeared from the curriculum of many modern schools. By dropping Bible reading they have been robbed of a rich resource. Within its pages may be found history, poetry, prophecy, and wisdom literature, as well as the gospels, the Acts, and the letters of St Paul. Its language is noble, and its contents are uplifting. They are morally and spiritually formative. Of the time when Britain was truly great, an eminent historian testified:

> When Elizabeth came to the throne, the Bible and Prayer Book formed the intellectual and spiritual foundation of a new social order. (G. M. Trevelyan)

TRUTH LIES IN THE TEACHER

However good the quality of the resource material, it is only as good as the teacher using it. The pupil is impressed more by the character of his teacher than by books. Truth lies in people. The apostles spoke of the truth 'as it is in Jesus'. His character was such that he could justly claim to be *'the way, the truth, and the life'*, and say to his disciples 'Follow me'. Especially does this apply when the subject to be taught is religion. When St Paul reminded Timothy of the Scriptures, he added 'knowing *of whom* thou hast learnt them. . .'. Timothy revered Paul as a teacher, but was reminded that his first teacher was his mother. The influence of good parents is paramount.

> When I call to remembrance the unfeigned faith that is in thee, which dwelt first in thy grandmother Lois, and thy mother Eunice; and I am persuaded that in thee also. (2 Timothy 1.5)

Faith is not so much taught as *caught*. The living flame is passed on from person to person, caught from the one in whom it burns. To give the task of teaching religious knowledge to an unbeliever is not only useless but also positively harmful. I remember the shock

I felt as a young child, when I heard an unbelieving schoolmaster ask to borrow a Bible, as he had never possessed nor read one; and yet had been asked to teach Scripture in the school. Imagine the damage he might inflict on young impressionable minds! It was to remedy this lack of suitable teachers that Church teacher-training colleges were founded; and it is important that churches should encourage candidates with a strong and living faith to fill them.

FAITH IN CHRIST

It is some years since I received a letter from a Christian schoolmaster which gladdened my heart. He recalled a dark winter's night a lifetime ago, when we stood together beneath a lamp-post in a northern city where we had once attended the same school. There we had been made to learn certain passages of Scripture and commit them to memory. It was not the best way to teach Scripture; but, as my former school friend said later, that night, under the lamp-post, the flame of faith was kindled by our conversation, and what had long slept in the memory was awakened. That night Harry found faith in Christ, and subsequently became a Christian schoolmaster. Years passed by, and then I received another letter telling me of his death. It was from an aged teacher he had befriended. She testified to his Christian faith, and told of many acts of kindness received at his hands. Then she added 'Dear Harry! At last he has entered into his glory'. I think I know what she meant, but I feel sure she got the date wrong; for Harry 'entered into his glory' forty years before, on the day he hitched his gown, picked up a piece of chalk, and entered the classroom as a schoolmaster for the first time!

LENT
Springtime Renewal

PRIDE AND PREJUDICE

It was springtime for Israel. The land was showing the green shoots of prosperity, and it was a time of great national pride. Israel boasted of being God's chosen people, and of having a King reputed to be the wisest man on earth! Under Solomon they had extended their frontiers, and gained great wealth. With it they had built a splendid temple to their God. On that very day it had been dedicated with great pomp and pageantry; so Solomon went to bed well pleased with himself. The Bible says he was 'prosperously effected' (see 2 Chronicles 7.11). But that night the Lord God appeared to him to give both a promise and a warning.

If my people, which are called by my name, shall humble themselves, and pray, and seek my face, and turn from their wicked ways; then will I hear from heaven, and will forgive their sin, and will heal their land . . . But if ye turn away, and forsake my statutes and my commandments, which I have set before you, and shall go and serve other gods, and worship them; Then I will pluck them up by the roots out of my land which I have given them; and this house, which I have sanctified for my name, will I cast out of my sight, and will make it to be a proverb and a byword among all nations. (2 Chronicles 7.14, 19–20)

PERVERSITY AND GRIEF

A couple of years ago, on a visit to modern Israel, the ancient warning came to mind as I stared at the Muslim mosque standing where the Jewish Temple once stood. Below it was the Wailing Wall, all that remained of the once splendid Temple; and by it stood a long line of wandering Jews who had returned in grief to beat their breasts and pray. All around was the scene of bitter strife between

35

Arab and Jew, often seen on world-wide television. Israel had become, as God had predicted, 'a byword among all nations'. The ruined Temple, the wandering Jew, and the Wailing Wall, remind all nations of what happens if they turn away from God, and disobey his commands.

Have you ever wondered why Scripture records the deeds of a bygone age, and the details of the Temple long-demolished? Why are the misdeeds of men and women long dead preserved in Holy Writ? Is it because God intends past mistakes to be remembered for future guidance? Is it to warn the present generation of the abiding consequence of forgotten sins? 'Whatsoever things were written aforetime were written for our learning' (Romans 15.4).

THE PRESENT PREDICAMENT

King Solomon was warned nearly three thousand years ago, but it was only in 1978 that Lord Hailsham wrote:

> For some years now . . . I have been oppressed by a sinister foreboding. We are living in the City of Destruction, a dying country in a dying civilization . . . One cannot go on indefinitely refusing to face the facts of life . . . It may be a slow slide to destruction, or it may all end in a big bang . . . but sooner or later, when a nation has lost is self-respect, there will come a time when it must face the truth. (*The Dilemma of Democracy*)

More recently, the Queen expressed to the Commonwealth a similar foreboding, if the nations of the world continue to ruin the environment on which we all depend for our existence; and in an oblique reference to the marital problems of the royal family she spoke of an *annus horribilis*. The newspapers tell of the tremendous rise in what they call 'crime', but the Bible calls 'sin'. The statistics of sin show a 16 per cent rise last year, and a doubling of misdeeds over the past twelve years. They show a national turning away from God, and a mass breaking of his commandments. So does what God said to Solomon three thousand years ago still apply to sinners today? How seriously should we take the divine warning? How stands the Word of God in this present time? What are the perilous consequences of breaking God's commandments? Can man get away with ignoring his Creator's commands? Will life still run smoothly if he forgets God? Motorists know that their car will grind to a halt if the maker's instructions are ignored; how much more then the life of man! How long can a nation survive after it has forgotten its faith? The Ten Commandments are seldom heard today, and are as seldom obeyed. God's warnings about wrongdoing may be muted, and sin given less serious names; but disease and death still follow in their train. 'The soul that sinneth it shall die' (Ezekiel 18.4).

PRESCRIPTION FOR RENEWAL

Both as a Church and as a nation, we have got ourselves into a sad state. The divine diagnosis is no less serious for being short—'*sin*!' Thank God, however, that besides the deadly diagnosis stands the divine cure—God's remedy for sin. It contains God's requirements for renewal.

If my people, which are called by my name, shall humble themselves, and pray, and seek my face, and turn from their wicked ways; then I will hear from heaven, and will forgive their sin, and will heal their land. (2 Chronicles 7.14)

God gives three conditions.

(1) *'If my people, which are called by my name, shall humble themselves.'*
The healing of the nation starts with God's people, those called by his name. It starts not at the House of Commons, but at the house of God. It begins not with the government but with the Church. It must start with those who profess and call themselves Christians. It begins with an act of repentant humility. Solomon's kingdom fell through sinful arrogance and pride; yet sometimes, the Church has tried to rival his pomp, pageantry, and sinful pride. It has turned its Popes into princes, enthroned its bishops, and inflated the pride of its 'priests'. Observe the splendour of their robes! Yet did not Jesus with the simplicity of a single flower shame the splendour of Solomon's array? How far have they with arrogance and pride departed from the example of the Prince of heaven, who humbled himself and took upon him the form of a servant? How far have they gone from the Saviour, who stooped to wash the disciples' feet? As for the laity, don't they, too, need to humble themselves: confess sinful pride, and lower them-

37

selves at the Saviour's feet? Haven't we all, in some measure, departed from the Holy One, meek and lowly in heart? Renewal starts with repentance! Only a Church humbled and repentant can hope to be renewed in the grace of God; and only a Church renewed can hope to bring about the spiritual healing of the land.

(2) Secondly, says God, you need to *'pray, and seek my face'*.
This involves much more than the recital of printed prayers. It means that we must earnestly seek the face of God. We need to approach Almighty God with a humble and penitent heart, with faith in his forgiveness. What is required is not the patter of an oft-repeated prayer, but the sincere cry of the heart to God. 'Oh, that I might know where I can find him' cries the thirsty soul. Having found him, or rather, having been found of him, we need to look up into his face and pray, 'Lord, what wilt thou have me to do?' We look up in readiness to do his will. Have you ever watched a sheepdog devotedly looking up into its master's face to discern his will? How much more should we fix our eager gaze upon God?

(3) The third requirement for spiritual renewal, says God, is that men must *'turn from their wicked ways'*.
We must humble our pride, seek God's face and *'turn'*. That is what is meant by conversion—a turning. In the face of God we see the anguish of the cross, and our sorrow for sin brings us to the cross-road. It is time to turn. It is conversion time, the time to turn 'from', 'to'. It is time to turn from the way of wickedness to the way of the Saviour. See how conversion transforms things! Take a cup which has been inverted. In this position it is empty and useless. Now *convert* it, turn it the right way up, and make it face heavenwards. Now it is ready for service, ready to be filled and used. So it is with us—turned away from God our lives are empty and useless. Yet, converted, we can be used in the service of man and God. God can renew us and fill our lives with his grace and goodness. Then shall we know the joy of sins forgiven, broken relationships restored, souls renewed. 'And I will heal their land', says God.

It is the springtime of renewal.

38

MOTHERING SUNDAY
Our Religious Roots

Jerusalem ... which is the mother of us all.
GALATIANS 4.26

Here are words to warn the heart. They brought tears to the eyes of Jewish patriots, when their capital city was under the rule of the Romans. Many of the former citizens had been sent away into exile and, like exiles of another age, found themselves unable to sing the songs of Zion in a strange land. Their hearts were in Jerusalem. To the big religious festivals, however, they were sometimes allowed to return and participate. Many travelled hundreds of miles by land and sea, and when they caught sight of the shining pinnacles of the Temple they wept for joy. Jerusalem reminded them of a more glorious past, and held hopes of a yet more glorious future when once more she would be free. Christians spoke of the new Jerusalem, (see Revelation 7.12), freed from sin and oppression, as the symbol and hope of heaven. This prompted St Paul to write:

Jerusalem which now is, and is in bondage with her children. But Jerusalem which is above is free, which is the mother of us all. (Galatians 4.25–26)

THE TRADITIONAL MOTHERING SUNDAY

Many centuries have passed since the Apostle penned these words, yet the phrase 'mother of us all' continues to stir the hearts of us all. Mothering Sunday has become increasingly popular, judging by the enormous number of Mother's Day cards sold for the occasion. Florists, too, find it gives a tremendous fillip to their trade. Everyone, it seems, decides to give flowers to Mother on her special day. Although taken out of context, the phrase 'mother of us all' moves people at a deep emotional level. In the days when working-class girls left Mother to go into service at the big house,

39

and their brothers left home to serve seven years as bound apprentices, Mothering Sunday came as a welcome break; for on that day their employers freed them to visit their parents at home. They looked forward to the special Sunday with much eagerness, and brought home presents for their parents—a traditional simnel cake baked by the daughter, or a wooden gift carved by the son. Additionally, they brought presents of sweets and flowers. What joy there was in the old home when the whole family came back together! Their first thought as a united family was to go together to the village church, and thank God. After all, it was there that the family first began. There Mother and Father had been married. To the house of God they had been brought to be baptized into the family of the Church. It was there they had been taught the family values of love and loyalty, and to regard themselves as members of an even greater family—the family of God. Reunited, they prayed together and praised God for all his goodness, especially thanking him for Mother and all her loving care. Many of these old customs continue to be observed on the fourth Sunday in Lent, and many a mother continues to wipe away tears of joy.

THE THREE Rs OF FAMILY LIFE

Three Rs should remind us of the deeper meaning of Mothering Sunday.

First, they remind us of our *family roots*. In this modern age, perhaps even more than in the age of bound apprenticeships, families are soon uprooted and scattered. Jobs for teenagers are few in Cornwall, where I live, and where young people have to leave their village in order to obtain higher education in the big cities. Often they have to travel far from home to find employment. Though necessary, it is sad to see the families scattered in this way, as soon as sons and daughters have reached a certain age. Life in the universities and large communities has a different order and often a lower moral standard from that of the home. The pressure to conform to the pattern of their peers is hard to resist. Parental warnings tend to be set aside or forgotten, often with disastrous moral consequences. But Mothering Sunday comes around each year with the reminder of one's family roots and thoughts of those who love and care. There's no place like home! And to return on Mothering Sunday strengthens the old ties of love and loyalty. They

40

hold fast when the fierce winds of temptation blow.

Secondly, Mothering Sunday reminds us of *family religion*. We need to be reminded of our family roots; and it is even more important to be reminded of our membership of the family of the Church. We need to be reminded of our baptismal vows, and given the opportunity to refresh our faith. To go back to the old church as a family is good for the soul, and brings to mind the things that ultimately matter most. When the Jewish exiles returned to Jerusalem, the sight that moved them most deeply was the vision of the Temple where for generations their ancestors had worshipped. On that holy mountain David once had built a stronghold against the heathen foes. There Solomon once built a house for the Lord. Within those ancient walls their forefathers had worshipped from age to age, and their faith had stood as strong as the mountain. So the sight of the city set on a hill stirred thoughts of their God in ages past, and renewed their hope in him for years to come. I vividly remember my own first sight of Jerusalem. We had arrived in the darkness of night to be accommodated at a hostel situated just across the valley from the Holy City. We arose early to stand on the terrace and look across the Kidron Valley to see the city. There in reality Jerusalem stood, just like the city I had seen in my dreams, its walls golden in the morning sun! I was deeply moved. Just across was the hill Abraham, with heavy heart, had climbed with his son, so long ago. There was the city David had built. There Jesus went at the age of twelve with his parents to worship — and there, not far away, was the green hill on which my Saviour died! Places have associations, memories, and religious roots. The thought of Jerusalem the mother of us all adds a deeper dimension to Mothering Sunday. It is deeply rooted in history, and it would be tragic if the modern Mothering Sunday were to become merely 'Mother's Day', with family religion forgotten. Remembered, or not, Jerusalem remains the mother of us all.

The third R for Mothering Sunday reminds us that it is also called 'Refreshment Sunday', because of the Gospel reading of how the hungry multitude was miraculously fed by Jesus. It is the tale of many folk hungry and far from home, for whom Jesus still has compassion. Among the crowd was a little lad whose mother had remembered to pack his lunch — five little loaves, and two small fishes. It was not much, the loaves were little more than buns, and the fishes not much bigger than sprats — but little as was the gift of the boy, yet placed in the hands of Jesus, it proved more than enough! It must have been miraculously blessed and multiplied, for after all the five thousand had been fed, the disciples filled twelve baskets with fragments of the five barley buns 'which remained over and above unto them that had eaten'. The story was followed by the teaching of Jesus on the bread of God which cometh down from heaven, and the promise 'he that cometh to me shall never hunger; and he that believeth on me shall never thirst' (see John 6). In the Service of Holy Communion his promise is renewed. 'Come unto me, all ye that travail and are heavy laden, and I will refresh you' (Matthew 11.28). In the days of hard working conditions, weary folk must often have returned to the old church on Mothering Sunday in need of refreshing. Often, as they stretched forth hands of faith to receive the crumb of blessed bread, they found that Christ still satisfies the hungry soul. Mothering Sunday has good grounds for being also known as 'Refreshment Sunday'.

So let Mothering Sunday be restored to its true name and original purpose. In these modern times when the family is under attack, let it hold firmly to its deep roots in religion. We need to look in faith towards the new 'Jerusalem . . . which is the mother of us all'.

PALM SUNDAY
Who Is This?

And when he was come into Jerusalem, all the city was moved,
saying, Who is this?
MATTHEW 21.10

Much of the merciful ministry of Jesus was done quietly without
wish for publicity. His Messiahship was kept incognito. But on
Palm Sunday Christ came out into the open. Three things charac-
terize his Palm Sunday procession.

1. IT WAS PUBLIC YET PEACEFUL

Public demonstrations in occupied countries were dangerous. The
Roman legionaries were ruthless in suppressing any suspected
threat to Caesar's rule. Therefore the first Palm Sunday procession
was carefully planned to be peaceful. The disciples of Jesus were
sent to a village near the Mount of Olives, where at the crossroads
they would find a young colt tied. They were to loose him and bring
him to Jesus and, if challenged, give the pre-arranged password—
'the Lord hath need of him'. The owner would then let him go. We
are told that as yet the donkey was untrained—'whereon yet never
man sat'. Nevertheless, apparently he meekly allowed Jesus to
mount and ride him. On hearing this story, a young stable-lad
exclaimed 'Jesus must have had wonderful hands!' The frisky young
colt seemed to *know* his master. Donkeys are proverbially stubborn,
often ridiculed for their appearance, but this one was proud to know
that 'the Lord hath need of him'. Despite all the palm-waving and
the excited shouts of the crowd, he calmly carried Christ down the
steep hill of Olivet, across the Kidron Valley, and into the busy city.
Another ass might have shied at the din, but not he. His was a proud
role that day.

43

Fools! for I also had my hour.
One far fierce hour and sweet;
There was a   shout about my ears,
And palms before my feet. (G. K. Chesterton)

The gospels go on to say:

A very great multitude spread their garments in the way; others
cut down branches from the trees, and strawed them in the way
. . . and [they] that went before, and that followed, cried,
saying – Blessed is he that cometh in the name of the Lord:
Blessed be the kingdom of our father David, that cometh in the
name of the Lord: Hosannah in the highest. (See Matthew 21,
Mark 11 and Luke 19)

Jesus was given the red-carpet treatment. It was a right royal procession; men marching, and the women and children dancing for
joy. So loud were the shouts of acclamation, that all the city was
stirred. The demonstration was not done in a corner. They marched
boldly through the city gates. When last in Jerusalem, I stood and
gazed at the Golden Gate. It has now been bricked-up; blocked,
they say, until the Messiah comes. But on that marvellous day he
did come; and one day he will come again in glorious majesty. At
that first coming all the city was stirred by the sound of Hosannahs
and the chanting of the crowd, 'Blessed be the king that cometh in
the name of the Lord'. A shock wave ran though Jerusalem. Fearing
brutal retaliation by Caesar's men, some of the Pharisees said
'Master, rebuke thy disciples'. But Jesus replied 'I tell you, if
these should hold their peace, the very stones would immediately
cry out!'

2. IT WAS MEEK YET MAJESTIC

Seen in the long perspective of Christianity, that first Palm Sunday
seems gloriously triumphant. Down the centuries it has become the
day to worship Jesus as king. Stirring hymns and anthems are sung,
and fronds of Palm adorn the day. It is his day of majesty – 'Our
God reigns!' But it didn't start that way. When climbing the steep
and stony path of Mount Olivet, I once met a man on a donkey
slowly picking his way down. He was dressed in a rough homespun
robe, and his head was swathed against the heat of the sun. The

44

donkey was very small, and the man's legs dangled not far from the ground. My mind went back two thousand years to picture Jesus on that path. The man was far from impressive. Why then did Jesus riding a donkey down that self-same road arouse such wild enthusiasm? What was significant to stir them so? Foreigners would hardly consider the sight of an unarmed man riding on a donkey much of a threat to the might of Rome! But the patriotic Jews, versed in the Scriptures, saw in Jesus that day the prophetic signs of the Messiah. Here was God's anointed Leader, the King who would come to deliver them, the One sent to save them. 'Tell ye the daughter of Sion, behold, thy king cometh unto thee, meek, sitting upon an ass, upon a colt, the foal of an ass' (Zechariah 9.9). *All the symbols of the Prince of Peace were there*—the colt of an ass, the banners of palm, the garments strewn in his royal way, and the massed shouts of Hosannah. ('God save the King!') It was Messianic: It was Kingdom-time: God had visited his people! Despite his peaceful approach, Christ seemed every inch a king.

> Ride on, ride on in Majesty
> In lowly pomp ride on to die;
> Bow thy meek head to mortal pain,
> Then take, O God, thy power, and reign. (H. H. Milman)

3. IT WAS PROVOCATIVE YET PREVAILING

The triumphant procession challenged the establishment, yet seemed destined to fail. Within a week the shouts of 'hosannah' had given place to cries of 'crucify!' It seemed so powerless and pathetic. Some commentators have made much of the fickleness of the crowd, which one day shouted 'hosannah!', and the next day 'crucify!' Others have pointed out that, according to the gospel accounts, there were *two different crowds*—'They that went before, and they that followed' (Mark 11.19). There was the crowd which had followed Jesus down the hill, praising God for all the mighty works they had seen (see Luke 19.37); and there was the crowd which, hearing the shouting, came forth from the city to see. Among the crowd which came down from the hill may have been the once blind Bartimaeus, and the healed lepers, and those who had once been lame, and many whose lives had been wonderfully blessed by the mercy of Christ. I can hardly imagine *them* crying 'crucify!' Nor would the women who watched and wept as Jesus went by carrying his cross. The crowd that cried 'crucify' was a mob with passions whipped-up by the bigoted religious leaders. It was a 'rent-a-mob' by those who saw Jesus as a threat to their established position and privileges. There was bribery, misrepresentation, and political 'wheeling and dealing' at work. Caiaphas, the scheming high priest, actually had the affrontry to propose on grounds of patriotism and expediency, that Jesus be made their scapegoat. '*It is expedient for us* that one man should die for the people, and that the whole nation perish not' (John 11.50).

Caiaphas spoke far more truly than he knew! God can make even the wrath of man turn to his praise. Jesus, did, indeed, die for the people; one man bore the sins of many. He carried our sins without the camp, to a green hill outside the city wall; and there by his sacrifice became not only the scapegoat of sinners, but also the Saviour of the world.

GOOD FRIDAY
Outside the City Wall

From that time forth began Jesus to show unto his disciples, how he must go unto Jerusalem, and suffer many things.

MATTHEW 16.21

There was a feeling of foreboding as the disciples followed Jesus from the green fields of Galilee towards the grim heights of Judaea and the city of Jerusalem. It stood like a fortress, high among the mountains of Moriah, guarded by strong walls overlooking the smoking valley of Hinnom, the hellish place where rubbish was burnt. Down the centuries, Jerusalem daunted the sight of many a foe, and even its friends had cause to weep over the city and its sin.

OUTSIDE THE CITY WALL

Today, outside the city wall is a busy bus-station, and nearby is the green hill which some suppose to be the site where Jesus was crucified. Actually, tourists are told of two possible sites of the crucifixion. The traditional site lies inside the present city-walls, within the church of the Holy Sepulchre. The other is outside the wall where people wait for transport. It is not difficult to imagine the nearby hill as Golgotha, for it is shaped like a skull, and two holes give the impression of eye sockets. The site is known as Gordon's Calvary for, in the beautiful garden near the base of the hill, General Gordon used to gaze at Golgotha and meditate upon the cross. The garden, also, intrigued him; believing it to be the original garden of the resurrection, he had it excavated. His exploration made two exciting discoveries. The first was an ancient tomb, similar to the one in which Jesus was laid. It had been hewn out of the rock face, and had a groove to guide the sealing-stone. Opinion about the authenticity of the site is divided among historians; but believers reverently remember what the Bible said about the site: 'Now in the place where he was crucified there was

47

a garden; and in the garden a new tomb, wherein was never man laid' (John 19.41).

THE WINEPRESS

Secondly, on the same site was uncovered an ancient winepress, which to Bible readers proves deeply significant. The book of Isaiah prophesied of One 'mighty to save', whose garments were stained with blood, and who had 'trodden the winepress alone' (Isaiah 63.3). It pictured a winepress and the traditional method of treading on the grapes, with the juice staining the garments of the worker. The scene was then transferred to the one 'mighty to save', treading the blood-stained way in the winepress of God. Alone he trod it, and he trod it *outside the city*.

The book of Revelation takes up the theme, and tells of the vine of the earth being gathered, and cast into 'the great winepress of the wrath of God' (against sin). 'And the winepress was trodden without the city, and blood came out of the winepress' (Revelation 14.20). When we remember that Jesus claimed to be the True Vine, the mystery deepens; for it is the only plant bound to a stake, that bleeds to bless!

THE ROCK

Dominating Jerusalem stands the historic Dome of the Rock, drawing pilgrims of the three main world religions in their thousands. To Muslims it is sacred because of the beautiful Mosque built over the place from which they believe their prophet ascended to heaven. To Jews it is sacred as the site on which Herod rebuilt the Temple of Solomon, and where there still stands, as a place of prayer, a section of one of the original walls (the Wailing Wall).

But Christians are drawn not only to the site of the Temple attended by Jesus, and the scene of many a gospel story; not merely to see the mosque which replaced it, but also to see the great rock itself. There, in the middle of the elaborately decorated mosque, rears-up the gaunt rock from the summit of Mount Moriah, the altar of rock to which Abraham led his dearly beloved son on that fateful day, two thousand years before Christ.

And it came to pass after these things, that God did test Abraham, and said unto him . . . Take now thy son, thine only son Isaac, whom thou lovest, and get thee into the land of Moriah; and offer him there for a burnt offering upon one of the mountains which I will tell thee of . . . And Abraham took the wood of the burnt offering, and laid it upon Isaac his son; and he took the fire in his hand, and a knife; and they went both together. And Isaac said, My Father . . . behold the fire and the wood: but where is the lamb for a burnt offering? And Abraham said, My son, God will provide himself a lamb . . . so they went, both of them together. (Genesis 22.1–8)

We remember that at the dramatic moment when the knife was raised and the son was offered, a cry was heard—the cry of a lamb caught in a thicket, the God-provided substitute for the dearly beloved son. Then we think of the greater sacrifice of Jesus, the Lamb of God that taketh away the sin of the world, and the offering of God's dearly beloved Son, the One for whom there is no substitute. Runnels on the rock carried away the blood of countless sacrifices, until finally Christ came to make the great sacrifice once and for all, and never to be repeated (see Hebrews 9.26).

THE HYMN

Why did Jesus have to die? Preachers of the cross have wracked their brains, and searched for illustrations to make plain the reason why. Some have dwelt on the sacrifice, some on the substitution, some on the battle with sin, while others have seen the cross as a divine demonstration of love. We leave it to the theologians to wrestle with the meaning of 'ransom', and 'propitiation'; and turn to the children's hymn which a great preacher has described as 'The most profound statement of the Atonement ever made' (Dr Leslie Weatherhead).

> There is a green hill far away,
> Without a city wall,
> Where the dear Lord was crucified,
> Who died to save us all.

Gounod considered it the most perfect hymn ever written in the English language, and set it to the tune we all know and love.

It was written for the children of the walled city of Londonderry in Northern Ireland, the scene of much bloodshed. Outside the city wall was a green hill, well known to the children. So when writing the hymn Mrs Alexander decided to make the hill of Calvary, though far away, as real to the children as the one they knew so well. She wanted to make the sacrifice of Jesus significant in their daily life. The original word 'without' confused the children, so she altered it to 'outside' a city wall.

Being spiritually wise, she made no attempt to explain the great mystery of the cross to the children's little minds; knowing that though some things are beyond one's mental grasp, yet they are within the reach of faith! A man's reach should always exceed his grasp!

> We may not know, we cannot tell.
> What pains He had to bear,
> But we believe it was for us
> He hung and suffered there.

To say 'Christ died for me' is the deepest expression of one's faith, and personally to realize that truth is the most profound perception one can ever make. It is life's most unforgettable experience. In the Second World War, a friend took the place intended for me, in an aircraft which burst into flames a few seconds after take-off. The sight of his badly burnt body stirred me beyond words; and the memory still does. What can we say of the One who has taken our place and suffered in our stead, except to stutter 'He died for me!' The death of my friend, so long as I live, can never be forgotten. But what shall we say of Christ's death, since we believe it was for us that he hung and suffered there?

The hymn says it all, and speaks for all of us.

> He died that we might be forgiven,
> He died to make us good.
> That we might go at last to heaven,
> Saved by His precious blood.
>
> O dearly, dearly has He loved,
> And we must love Him, too.
> And trust in His redeeming blood,
> And try His works to do. (Frances Alexander)

50

EASTER
Peter's Easter Sermon

We are witnesses of all things which Jesus did both in the land of the Jews, and in Jerusalem; whom they slew and hanged on a tree: Him God raised up the third day, and showed him openly.

ACTS 10.39, 40

A JOYOUS REALIZATION

For most of us Easter comes not a day too soon. After winter with its cold, dark, and depressing days, comes Easter; making the daffodils to dance, the sun to shine, and the congregation to smile. It is the happiest day in the Christian year. The tale is often told of old Dr Dale consulting his textbooks as he sat in his study preparing to deliver a scholarly sermon on Easter day. Suddenly he sprang up and exclaimed 'He is alive! Christ is risen!' His eyes at that moment of realization were opened to the glorious fact that at Easter Christ broke-out not only from the tomb, but also from the barrier of time, itself. The risen Christ had shown himself not merely as a fact of history, but as an eternal fact! Easter was, and is, a timeless event. Christ is gloriously risen and alive, today! As Dale paced up and down his study, the wonder of it all dawned on his soul. No longer could he continue to preach ponderously, and tediously present details of an event in history. He would present the risen Christ as alive, and with them that very day! Standing in the pulpit, he put aside his prepared notes, raised his arms, and with all the excitement of his discovery exclaimed 'Christ is risen! Christ is risen!' He then shut the book, came down from the pulpit, and announced the Easter anthem. It was the shortest and most effective sermon the startled congregation had ever heard preached.

(How many another long-suffering congregation must wish their preacher would do the same!) For a brief account of one of the most powerful sermons ever delivered, preached by no less a person than St Peter, himself, read Acts 10.34–44.

THE EAGERNESS OF HIS CONGREGATION

Of course, the apostle was fortunate in having the ideal sort of congregation, of which every preacher dreams; prepared, and gathered together at Divine instigation. This was no ordinary congregation, brought by habit to participate in a formal act of worship; but a gathering eager to receive through the apostle the word of God. Cornelius, the Roman centurion, had been stirred by a heavenly vision to send for Peter, and was divinely moved to gather his entire household and friends, in anticipation of the visit of God's messenger. When the apostle arrived he found an ideal congregation already assembled, eagerly waiting to hear what God had given his messenger to say. By way of introduction, Cornelius told the assembly of his vision, and how God had commanded him to send for the apostle. He then turned to Peter saying 'Now therefore are we all here present before God, to hear all things commanded thee of God' (Acts 10.33). It would have warmed the cockles of any preacher's heart!

THE CORE OF HIS MESSAGE

Straightway, Peter plunged into the heart of his message and told them about Jesus – 'Who went about doing good, and healing all who were oppressed'. He spoke of the compassion of Christ for the sick, the sad, and the sinful; and then swiftly he came to the crux of his sermon. He spoke of the crucifixion of Jesus, 'whom they slew and hanged on a tree'. They could not believe their ears. A good man, crucified? Impossible! That terrible death was reserved for the worst of men. No Roman citizen was ever put to such shame; and even the Jews said 'Accursed be the man who hangs upon the tree'.

If a Roman governor had imposed such a shameful penalty, then Jesus must not have been good! That execution by crucifixion had nailed the false claim that Jesus was a good man who went about doing good. 'Christ crucified' shamed Christianity, exposed its falsity, and made nonsense of the Gospel message. How could such bring salvation? At this stage of the sermon they were more than ready to reject the message, and who can blame them? A dead Christ is not Good News. The preaching of the cross, if it stops there, is foolishness. That is not the Gospel of Christ. Although Paul said 'We preach Christ crucified . . .' he did not stop there;

nor did Peter. It was not the full Gospel. Good Friday would remain Bad Friday, without Easter Day. The empty cross and the empty tomb, not the crucifix, tell the Good News that Christ is risen. Without the empty tomb the cross would be a dreadful catastrophy for Christianity. So Peter went on: 'Him God raised up the third day!' Had a television camera been present to focus on the faces of that congregation, it would have highlighted looks of astonishment and disbelief. 'Dead men tell no tales! Don't ask us to believe such a tale. When a man is dead he is stone-dead, and none ever came back from the dead to tell any different.'

THE CONVICTION OF HIS WITNESS

Some might have been ready to argue with the apostle, although he wasn't there to argue his case, but to convince by his personal witness. To be able to witness was essential to apostleship. They had to be men who could tell of Christ by personal experience. They had to be able to speak of things they had heard with their own ears, and seen with their own eyes, and experienced in their own lives. In filling the vacancy left by the defection of Judas it was specified that the apostle be chosen from

> men which have companied with us all the time that the Lord Jesus went in and out among us, beginning from the baptism of John, unto the same day that he was taken up from us, must one be ordained to be a witness with us of his resurrection. (Acts 1.21, 22)

It was with all the assurance and conviction of a chosen witness, of one who had actually met with the risen Christ, that Peter preached his Easter message:

> Him God raised up the third day, and showed him openly; not to all the people, but unto witnesses chosen before of God, even to us, who did eat and drink with him after he rose from the dead. (Acts 10.40–41)

He probably told of the mysterious stranger who had walked and talked with two disciples on the Emmaus road after the crucifixion; and how he had warmed their hearts by showing the suffering of the Saviour predicted by the prophets; and how, invited to share the evening meal, the risen Christ had revealed himself at the breaking of bread.

Moreover, said Peter, in the upper room, even as the Emmaus disciples ran back to tell us, Jesus stood among us, revealing himself to the eleven and those who were with them.

> and while they believed not for joy . . . he said to them, Have you here any meat? And they gave him a piece of broiled fish, and of an honeycomb. And he took it, and did eat before them. (Luke 24.40–43)

Thoroughly warming to his sermon, the apostle went on, saying that he appeared to us again as we ate *by the side of the lake*. We had been fishing all night, without success, said Peter, and were cold and hungry, and our spirits were low. Then, by the shore we saw a stranger, or so he seemed in the morning mist; and there was a fire, and the smell of cooking. John recognized him as the Lord. The stranger said 'Come and dine'. What an awesome meal that was! We ate in reverent silence. We were too awed to speak, knowing that it was the Lord. That was no ordinary meal. It was Holy Communion! Holy were the hands that prepared it. Holy were the hands that lit the fire and cooked the food. The hands that blessed the bread bore the nail-prints!

> This was now the third time that Jesus showed himself to his disciples, after that he was risen from the dead. (John 21.14)

THE CONVERSION OF HIS HEARERS

It was a tremendous Easter message! It was a sermon on which the Holy Spirit set his seal. It is on record that 'While Peter yet spake these words, the Holy Ghost fell on all them which heard the word' (Acts 10.44). With the consequence that they believed, and were baptized and not only they! Whenever the risen Christ is preached, he stands among us; and the Holy Spirit sets his seal on the sermon. The Easter message breaks through the barrier of the passing centuries, as Christ once broke through the tomb. The message is timeless. As the hymn says – it is 'the Eternal Easter-tide'. The risen Christ left behind the trappings of the tomb, to stride out into life, to cross the continents, and to share that eternal life with all who believe.

Even now, as we attend the Easter service of Holy Communion, he reaches out to you and me. He invites us to share with him the sacred meal, and to commune with him now, as did those of old 'who did eat and drink with him after he rose from the dead' (Acts 10.41).

As he reaches out towards us in love, so let us reach out towards him in faith. As we share the bread, and drink the wine, may our eyes be opened to his risen presence, and accept with grateful hearts the benefits of his redeeming love. Pray that the Holy Spirit which fell on that congregation then, may now fall on us, today.

ROGATIONTIDE
Industrial Sunday

Study to show thyself approved unto God, a workman that needeth not to be ashamed.

2 TIMOTHY 2.15

PRAYING FOR THE WORKER

Rogations (processional prayers) have long been associated with the custom of 'beating the bounds of the parish', and asking God's blessing on the workers in the fields. After the Industrial Revolution, however, rogations were said not only for the workers in the fields, but also for workers in the factories and 'dark Satanic mills'. Industrial Sunday was first observed in 1920, when special services were held on the Sunday preceding 1 May (Labour Day). The manual worker was esteemed in the New Testament. St Paul earned his living by working as a tent-maker, so that his ministry should be without charge on the Church. In this context he may have been advising Timothy to do likewise; although the primary reference is to the work of preaching and teaching the Gospel, 'rightly dividing the word of truth'.

WORSHIP AND THE WORKSHOP

It is significant that, although at the age of twelve Jesus said 'I must be about my father's business', he spent the next eighteen years in the workshop of Nazareth. Only the last three years of his life were devoted to the work of an itinerant teacher. Should his desire to be about his 'Father's business' have been spelt with a small or a capital F? Tradition says that Joseph was a good deal older than Mary, and that when he died, the responsibility of providing for the widow and young family rested on Jesus, the apprentice he had trained. If this tradition were true, then perhaps Jesus believed his duty, for the time being, was to be about his *earthly* father's business.

The ambition to be a Rabbi had to be shelved for a while. It was while he was working in the carpenter's shop that he hammered out the Christian doctrine of work. Jesus studied to be a good workman, as accurate in cutting wood as in rightly dividing the word of truth. Dr T. R. Glover, in his study of this period of Christ's life, wrote:

> There was one workshop in Nazareth where benches were made to stand firmly on four legs, doors made to open and shut properly, and where ploughs and yokes were fashioned to a perfect fit. (*The Jesus of History*)

No shoddy workmanship ever came out of that carpenter's shop. He made yokes smooth, in consideration of the beasts that had to bear them. He made ploughs that would run true. His chairs were designed to rest the weary and ease the heavy-laden. He did his work superbly well to serve both man and beast, and in so doing showed himself 'approved unto God'. Work and worship were not separated. Whether in the synagogue or the workshop his concern was to honour God. The prayers of his lips and the labour of his hands were complementary.

His life was perfect and of one piece. When finally the task of supporting the family was completed, Jesus locked the workshop door and went out to do his *heavenly* Father's business—teaching and healing, and working out man's full salvation by wood and nails on the cross. At his death he truly claimed 'It is finished. I have finished the work thou gavest me to do.'

GOD'S WORK AND OURS

As time moved on from the days of craftsmanship to the conveyor-belt and methods of mass production, men lost the spiritual purpose of work. Much of their work became dull and repetitive; and some would say soul-destroying. Much of their life was spent in mills and factories, where is it hard to find any purpose in working, apart from the need to earn a living. If the Gospel of Christ is to mean anything in the modern work-place, it must take account of the convictions Jesus hammered-out in his workshop; but can the ancient Scriptures bring meaning into the chaos of contemporary life? The Bible begins by showing *God* at work. The Word of God was at work bringing light out of darkness, order out of chaos, and life out of deadness. Seven periods of time are shown, six of which were working days. On the seventh, says Scripture 'God rested'; but did he cease working for ever? Jesus said 'My Father worketh until now, and I work' (John 5.17). The Divine Activity went on, work which Jesus was privileged to share. If God works, so should we! It is more than a means of earning a living: it is divine service. To work in support of one's children, to feed and clothe the weak, is to co-operate in the work of Divine Providence. Work well done, and from the right motive, dignifies even the most menial job. Who can forget the spectacle of Jesus washing the disciples' feet?

'Six days shalt thou *labour*' was God's commandment (see Exodus 20.9); but, if these words are to make sense in this present age of automation, 'labour' will have to be reinterpreted. Dull laborious work looks more like a curse than a blessing. Creative work is in a different category, and service given for God spells both soul-satisfaction and benefit to the community. It was the work of serving mankind that Jesus meant when he said my heavenly Father worketh until now, and I work. He linked his labours with God's continued work of love in the world he had made. I like the comment of a former Dean of St Paul's, when talking to a workmen engaged in the redecoration of the Cathedral.

'What is your trade?'

'Only a painter and decorator, sir'.

'How long have you been doing this kind of work?'

'Over forty years, sir.'

'Think of it! Forty years of making places sweet, fresh, and beautiful!' exclaimed the Dean. 'Why, it's Divine work!'

We need to see the spiritual significance in what men mistakenly call 'the common things of life'. When Jesus looked around his workshop, he saw many common things, later used as parables — a plough brought in for repair, cracked by carelessness when a man looked back and hit against a boulder, and an ill-fitting yoke someone had neglected to shape to the oxen's neck! 'No man, having put his hand to the plough, and looking back, is fit for the kingdom of God' (Luke 9.62). 'My yoke is easy, and my burden is light' (Matthew 11.30). On his bench lay two estimates, one for a bigger barn, and the other for a coffin — both for the same man! 'Thou fool, this night thy soul shall be required of thee'! (Luke 12.20). Jesus saw in the so-called 'common things of life' the signs and symbols of eternal life. He saw his work as service to God and man. His skill was devoted to doing all things well; as did God in the work of creation, see, for example, Genesis 1.31. In working for the good of the community, Jesus obeyed God's command to love one's neighbour. His teaching applies not only to work-people, but also to Christian employers. The garden cities of Bourneville and Port Sunlight prove Christ's principles can be applied in the modern world.

ASCENSION DAY
Two Worlds Are Ours

SYMBOLS AND COMMONSENSE

On the walls of the ancient church of St Austell, Cornwall, is a series of emblemic shields, depicting some of the main features of the Christian faith. Tourists inspecting the symbol of Christ's Ascension sometimes look either puzzled, or sceptical; for only the lower edge of a garment and two feet are shown, lifted a little above the ground. In this modern space age it seems to make no sense; yet, for the past seven hundred years, it has served as an effective sermon in stone. Successive generations have 'read' the symbol, and its message has got through even to the illiterate. However, in our matter-of-fact world, some have lost the sense of imaginative metaphor and figurative expression. Religious symbols no longer stir their mind and imagination. They see them as pictures of the past, instead of windows into the world of eternity. Many have lost the ability to interpret the spiritual symbolism of another world; and yet their imagination is stirred by the stories of space fiction. Fiction seems to be preferred to faith. With eyes fixed on fiction they are blind to the fact and meaning of Christ's Ascension. One wants to put to them the question addressed to the first disciples:

> Ye men of Galilee, why stand ye gazing up into heaven? this same Jesus, which is taken up from you into heaven, shall so come in like manner as ye have seen him go into heaven ... Then returned they unto Jerusalem from the mount called Olivet. (Acts 1.11–12)

On the Mount of Olives pilgrims are shown another symbol. It is merely of a mark on the ground; but it has been reverenced down the centuries as the last footprint of Christ on earth, marking the place from which Jesus ascended into heaven. Down the centuries it has been kissed by thousands of pilgrims. Today, however, it is protected by framed glass within a round tower, the Chapel of the Ascension (now a Muslim mosque). Sceptics see but a depression preserved in the sun-baked earth,

60

but believers see an impression of the Saviour's feet, and are stirred to pray:

> Grant, we beseech thee, Almighty God, that like as we do believe thy only-begotten Son our Lord Jesus Christ to have ascended into the heavens; so we may also in heart and mind thither ascend, and with him continually dwell, who liveth and reigneth with thee and the Holy Ghost, one God, world without end. Amen. (*Book of Common Prayer*)

SCIENCE AND SCEPTICISM

People have long since ceased to think of the earth as a flat disc with overarching sky, and heaven hidden behind the clouds. Ever since the time of Copernicus and Galileo, scientists have stretched our mental horizons. They have managed to land a man on the Moon, and have begun to probe the mysteries of outer-space. Concurrently, modern men have found it harder to see significance in the ancient symbols of religion (although one astronaut who landed on the moon was converted by the experience!). Sceptics there have been in every age. In the first century the Apostle Paul exclaimed:

> The natural man receiveth not the things of the Spirit of God: for they are foolishness unto him; neither can he know them, because they are spiritually discerned. (1 Corinthians 2.14)

Much of the Bible is expressed in poetry and parable, sign and symbol. In religion, as in mathematics, symbols are needed to express truth. Some things can be expressed in no other way. Try algebra without symbols! Stephen Hawking, one of the the world's most brilliant theoretical physicists, had to use symbols, when from his wheelchair, he tried to reach outer-space and come to terms with the mystery of the created universe. He found himself in a region of unknown dimensions. It was a mysterious realm, and needed to be approached with due humility, as his book (*A Brief History of Time*) concluded: 'If we find an answer to that, it would be the ultimate triumph of human reason—for then we would know the mind of God!'

MEN OF TWO WORLDS

Heavenly hope and human bewilderment arise from belonging to *two* worlds—the world visible, and the world unseen. Though proud to be a Roman citizen, St Paul claimed that his true citizenship was in heaven. We, too, have that dual citizenship, and on our earthly pilgrimage rely on symbols to signpost us to the heavenly city. We glimpse the glory of God in the human face of Jesus; for he alone is the perfect similitude of the unseen God, 'the express image of his person' (Hebrews 1.3). He, supremely, is The Man of Two Worlds, and the true and living Way to unseen realms above. By proverb, parable, and the example of his perfect life, he signposted the way.

> Two worlds are ours: 'tis only sin
> Forbids us to descry
> The mystic heaven and earth within,
> Plain as the sea and sky. (John Keble)

The Heavenly Word made flesh realized how hard it was for earthbound creatures to comprehend the things of God; so he took the things of earth and made of them symbols of heaven, sacraments of things unseen. By bread and wine he gave to earthlings a foretaste of the heavenly banquet. By wood and nails he worked man's full salvation. Using human language he conveyed the truth of God. Finally, he gave to the watching disciples a lesson they would never forget. It was a dramatized parable of the Ascension, enacted before their very eyes, until 'a cloud received him out of their sight'. It marked the end of one era and the start of another, when men would 'walk by faith and not by sight'.

> And when he had spoken these things, while they beheld, he was taken up; and a cloud received him out of their sight. (Acts 1.9)

THE SIGNIFICANCE OF THE ASCENSION

Three tremendous truths follow from the Ascension.

1. *The crowning of Christ*

The Ascension reveals Christ raised to the highest estate. 'Up' signifies exaltation. The realm of England recognizes three estates,

'The Lords Spiritual, the Lords Temporal, and the Commons'. Life Peers come 'up' from the Commons; but Christ at the Ascension was raised to the highest estate of all—'King of Kings, Lord of Lords, the only Ruler of Princes'. He sits at God's right hand, and from his exalted state beholds all the dwellers upon earth. Bethlehem marked Christ's descent from heaven to a lowly estate; and Bethany his ascent to glory. Ascension Day was his coronation day!

> Wherefore God also hath highly exalted him, and given him a name which is above every name: That at the name of Jesus every knee should bow . . . And that every tongue should confess that Jesus Christ is Lord. (Philippians 2.9–11)

2. *The commissioning of his Church*

From the crowned Christ came the commission of his Church. It was both a missionary mandate and a royal charter. It conveyed authority from the throne-room of heaven. He who gave the missionary command and commission was the One to whom all power in heaven and on earth had been committed.

> Jesus came and spake unto them, saying, All power [authority] is given unto me in heaven and in earth. Go ye therefore, and teach all nations, baptizing them in the name of the Father, and of the Son, and of the Holy Ghost: Teaching them to observe all things whatsoever I have commanded you: and, lo, I am with you alway, even to the end of the world. (Matthew 28:18–20)

Endowed with this authority, the apostles went forth as ambassadors and heralds of the heavenly kingdom. They were commissioned to continue Christ's work, preach his Gospel, and call men of all nations to accept him as Saviour and Lord.

3. *The confirming of his Word*

Thirdly, the Ascension endorsed the preaching of the Gospel 'with signs following'. The phrase comes from the footnote to St Mark's gospel. One of the oldest copies of St Mark's gospel broke off incongruously with 'Neither said they anything to any man; for they were afraid'. What happened? Was the scribe interrupted? Did Nero's police suddenly seize the writer? Was the brittle manuscript broken and the original ending lost? We can only guess, but it is certain that the gospel did not end with silence and fear. In no way would that match the heroism of the 'glorious company of the apostles'! The inspired footnote states that wherever the apostles went the presence of the Lord went with them, working with them 'confirming the word with signs following' (Mark 16.20).

Freed from the limitations accepted at Bethlehem, the ascended Christ was no longer bound by space or time. The man of Galilee had become the Saviour of the whole wide world! Perhaps the finest confirmation of this is to be found in David Livingstone's missionary journal. It was penned at nightfall in darkest Africa when, surrounded by hostile savages, he was once tempted to abandon his mission and steal away under cover of darkness. However, having entered his latitude and longitude, and read his Bible, he wrote:

> January 14, 1856. Evening. Felt much turmoil of spirit in prospect of having all my plans knocked on the head by savages tomorrow. But I read that Jesus said 'All power is given unto me in heaven and in earth. Go ye therefore, and teach all nations, and lo, I am with you always, even unto the end of the world.' *It is the word of a gentleman of the most strict and sacred honour,* so there's an end of it. I will not cross furtively tonight . . . I feel quite calm now, thank God!

The Lord was working with him, and confirming his Word with signs following—sinners were converted, the sick were healed, ignorance was enlightened, and slavery smitten.

> So then after the Lord had spoken unto them, he was received up into heaven, and sat at the right hand of God. And they went forth, and preached everywhere, the Lord working with them, and confirming the word with signs following. Amen. (Mark 16.19–20)

WHITSUNTIDE
What's in a Name?

THE NAME PREFERRED?

Although the biblical word Pentecost has now replaced Whitsunday in the Church calendar, old people are nostalgic for the popular Whitsun of their younger days. They have happy memories of the church festival and the 'Whit Walks' of Christian witness. White dresses were worn on 'White Sunday,' and by the girls who held ribbons to the church banners carried on the 'Whit Walks'. Hundreds of parishioners marched behind the town band to the traditional Field day which marked the beginning of the national holiday. It was an occasion celebrated by music and dancing, children's games, and refreshments served on the field. So long were some of the processions that two bands were needed, one to lead and one to bring up the rear. It was not only a happy occasion, but also an impressive occasion of witness in the open air. That was, of course, before the politicians decided to make 1 May (Labour Day) a Bank Holiday, and fixed the last Monday of May as Spring Bank Holiday. This accelerated the process by which the the holiday became secular. The traditional customs associated with the religious festival lost their popularity, and the processions became fewer until eventually the Whit Walks ceased. The name Whitsun had lost its religious significance. No longer were white dresses worn on White Sunday, and the name of Pentecost replaced it in the church calendar.

Pentecost was the biblical name for the Jewish festival celebrated fifty days after the Passover, to commemorate the giving of the Law on Mount Sinai, and the ingathering of the first fruits of harvest. To Christians, Pentecost is the commemoration of the outpouring of the Holy Spirit on the early Church, and the first great ingathering of souls when St Peter preached his powerful sermon on that tremendous day. Inspired by the Holy Spirit, the disciples witnessed to a great multitude 'out of every nation under heaven . . . and there were added unto them about three thousand souls' (Acts 2.41).

Although some regret the passing of the old-time associations of Whitsun, yet others have been gladdened to find that the resurrected name of Pentecost has spelt new spiritual life to the Church of modern times. The tremors of that historic event are now being felt again in this present age. The wind of the Spirit is again moving across the great continents of the world. The inflow of converts on that first Pentecost is surpassed by the vast numbers being brought to Christianity in some parts of the world today. In some emergent nations converts are being brought into the Christian fellowship faster than churches can be built to house them. The old established churches of the West are astonished at the way Pentecostal faith is sweeping across Latin America, Africa, and the Philippines. The Third Person of the Trinity has come to the fore. Although the doctrine of the Holy Spirit has been acknowledged in the creeds and hymns down the centuries, the realization of the Spirit's influence has seldom been so strong as in the life of the Church today.

THE POWER CONFERRED

After the experience of Pentecost the Apostles were wonderfully changed. Lambs became lions! The cowardly became courageous. The reticent became outspoken; and the hesitant became confident in their testimony to Christ. Where formerly they had gathered behind locked doors, for fear of enemies, now they came out boldly to face the crowds, and confess faith in the risen Christ. It was as though they had been lifted physically, mentally, and spiritually. They were on so great a 'high' in their articulate enthusiasm and increased energy that men thought they had been imbibing new wine. In truth they *were* intoxicated, *God-intoxicated*, and filled with joy at their new-found spiritual power. In trying to illustrate the tremendous thing that had happened when the Holy Spirit came at Pentecost, St Luke in Acts, chapter 2, referred to two powerful sources of energy, the mighty elements of wind and fire.

1. *Wind*

And suddenly there came a sound from heaven as of a rushing mighty wind, and it filled all the house where they were sitting. (Acts 2.2)

The disciples gathered at Pentecost with one accord to pray for the promised Spirit of power. Jesus had told them to tarry in Jerusalem, where 'ye shall receive power when the Holy Spirit is come upon you'. So they gathered together, a hundred and twenty of them, probably in the same large upper room as that used for the Last Supper. Despite the size of the room it must have been hot and stifling behind locked doors and shuttered windows. Not a breath of air moved until suddenly they heard a supernatural sound, as of 'a rushing mighty wind'. It must have been supernatural for, despite the shuttered windows, it entered and filled all the house where they were sitting. It was a Divine wind, a wind from Heaven. It was the life-giving breath of God, his almighty answer to their fervent prayers. It was the power Jesus had promised, invisible, yet dynamic. They heard its sound and felt its might, recognizing it as the Spirit of God. (In the Hebrew language 'wind' and 'Spirit' are the same word.) It was the same Wind or Spirit that had empowered the prophets; and now it shook and entered the house. The stale atmosphere was dispelled, and the disciples were awakened to newness of life. They were revitalized by the breath of God. It was spiritual resuscitation, the divine kiss of life. They were filled with the Spirit, empowered to become 'the glorious company of the apostles'; and then sent out to overcome the evil might of Rome. In this our Decade of Evangelism we, too, need to pray

> Breathe on me, breath of God,
> Fill me with life anew.
> That I may love what thou dost love,
> And do what thou wouldst do. (E. Hatch)

2. *Fire*

And there appeared unto them cloven tongues like as of fire, and it sat upon each of them. (Acts 2.3)

Fire symbolized God's spiritual energy at work within them. It is an active word. The Greek word for fire is used in *purify*. It burns away the dross. The leaping flames bring warmth and light. The power of fire drives great ships, as does the wind. Fire is elemental energy, and the active principle of God was at work in the world. Moses sensed it when he gazed upon the burning bush. Fire flared from Mount Sinai when God's Law was given.

The earth shook, the heavens also dropped at the presence of God: even Sinai itself was moved at the presence of God. (Psalm 68.8)

It was a mysterious Cloud of Fire that divinely led the tribe of Israel through the desert, after their deliverance from Egypt. It was the fire of God that fell upon the altar of Elijah, when he confounded prophets of Baal. The Old Testament closed with the prediction that God's messenger would come like a 'refiner's fire' (Malachi 3.2).

John the Baptist opened the New Testament era with the proclamation that Christ would 'baptize with the Holy Wind and with fire' (see Matthew 3.11); and when Pentecost was fully come the fire fell on God's people at prayer. The flames leapt like living things, dividing into tongues of fire, flickering above the heads of the believers, to inspire and energize them to carry on the work of Christ. Kindled in them was a burning zeal to preach the Gospel and forward his kingdom.

The early disciples had an experience . . . that for ever calcined to ashes their selfishness, their cowardice, their love of ease, and made them fight like tigers for Jesus Christ. (Eva Stuart Watt, *Thirsting for God*)

THE DIVINE PERSON WELCOMED

The metaphors of wind and fire only partially express what the disciples experienced at Pentecost. The Holy Spirit is not just a power but a Person—the third Person of the Divine Trinity. The apostles welcomed him into their midst as an invisible Presence. It was as Jesus had promised, 'Where two or three are gathered together in my name, there am I in the midst'. He was the Spirit of holiness, the *alter ego* of Jesus, who had promised to be with them always. He was the Invisible Companion to accompany them on their world mission. He, the Holy Spirit, was the Divine Guest who had come to dwell among them, and be in them; for the Holy Spirit of Jesus was not just a powerful force, but a dynamic Person. Jesus called him the Paraclete, the Divine Helper, the Spirit of Holiness who would come to remind them of the things of Christ, and dwell in them to empower, encourage, and purify. His influence would produce in them the fruits of the Spirit, and the Church would be advanced by his power.

St Peter in his pentecostal sermon made it clear that spiritual power was not to be confined to apostolic times; but that we, in our time, might expect the Divine Guest to knock on our door.

This is that which was spoken by the prophet Joel; And it shall come to pass in the last days, saith God, I will pour out my Spirit upon all flesh . . . repent, and be baptized every one of you in the name of Jesus Christ for the remission of sins, and ye shall receive the gift of the Holy Ghost. *For the promise is unto you, and to your children, and to all that are afar off, even as many as the Lord our God shall call.* (Acts 2.16–17, 38–39)

So let us by faith respond to that call, open the door, and welcome the Divine Guest into our lives.

TRINITY SUNDAY
A Sermon in Stone

*The grace of our Lord Jesus Christ, and the love of God, and the
fellowship of the Holy Spirit be with you all.*

2 CORINTHIANS 13.14 (RSV)

THE THREEFOLD SYMBOL

For ten years I was vicar of Holy Trinity church, St Austell,
Cornwall. Soon after appointment I was told that it was customary
to hold an annual civic service on Trinity Sunday; and that I would
be expected to preach frequently on the doctrine of the Trinity in
relation to the life of the town. I had heard very few sermons on
the Trinity (which may explain why I was found sitting on the steps
of the market hall gazing up fixedly at the church tower, directly
opposite). The tower bears a representation of the Divine Trinity,
which is said to be 'one of the sights most worth seeing in Cornwall'
(A. L. Rowse). It is described as a fine example of Italianate art,
but for me it proved a sermon in stone. It gave substance to a
difficult and abstract doctrine.

The artist embodied the idea of Father, Son, and Holy Spirit in
substantial stonework. The Divine Father he represented as seated
on the throne of heaven, supporting the cross on which hangs God's
dearly beloved Son. The third Person of the Trinity was originally
represented by a dove; but fierce storms over the centuries have
worn away the symbol. Appropriately, despite restoration of the
stonework of the church, the Holy Spirit has been left invisible. My
meditation on the representation in stone impressed on me three
things when preaching. One, never attempt to talk in abstract terms,
but rather give them substance. Two, appeal to the eye—make much
use of symbols and word-pictures. Three, make sure the message
gets down to the market-place.

For more than seven hundred years the church has stood in the
centre of the town. I wondered how many hundreds of thousands
of people in passing had glanced up to check the time on the church

clock, and then been reminded of the eternal Trinity—Father, Son, and Holy Spirit.

THE THREEFOLD WEAVE

Incidentally, have you ever wondered about the frequent occurrence of the number *three* in nature, life, and literature? The world consists of earth, sea, and sky. Man is body, mind, and spirit. His faculties are thinking, feeling, and willing. Time speaks of past, present, and future. The Scriptures frequently mention three—three temptations in the wilderness; three tabernacles are suggested on the Mount of Transfiguration; three times Jesus prayed in Gethsemane; and the denials of Peter were three. There were three crosses on Calvary. The resurrection took place on the third day. The Ter-Sanctus, the threefold song of the Seraphim—Holy, Holy, Holy—is central to the Eucharist; and most acts of worship conclude with the threefold blessing of Father, Son, and Holy Ghost. The Trinity seems to be woven into the tapestry of life; and yet the three main religions of the world are monotheistic. One God is worshipped, not three. Those brought up in the religion of Judaism are from childhood taught that the Lord our God is but One: 'Him only shalt thou serve'. The Muslims make the same strict emphasis. I remember watching the Muslims at prayer in the walled Muslim city of Kano, northern Nigeria. Daily they chanted, as they prostrated themselves in prayer, 'There is but *one* God, *one* God, *one* God; and Muhammad is his prophet'.

Christianity, too, notwithstanding belief in the Trinity, is strongly monotheistic. The Thirty-nine Articles of Religion affirm 'There is but *one* living and true God . . .' The Nicene Creed begins 'I believe in *one* God, the Father Almighty . . .' and then goes on to say 'and in one Lord Jesus Christ . . .', adding 'And I believe in the Holy Ghost . . .' The Athanasian Creed states that belief in the Trinity is essential to salvation; yet, neither the Articles of Religion, nor the Creeds of the Church, contradict the oneness of God. The first Christians were Jewish, brought up to believe in the one true God. They, like all Jews and Muslims, were drilled to repeat 'I believe in the 'one God, one God, one God'; and feared the blasphemy of believing in any other God.

71

THE THREEFOLD EXPERIENCE

How then did belief in the Divine Trinity come to be affirmed by
Jewish Christians? As we read the gospels we detect in those closest
to Jesus a growing belief that he was more than man. 'We beheld
His glory . . . full of grace and truth', said John. 'Lord, to whom
shall we go? Thou hast the words of eternal life', said Peter. 'My
Lord, and my God!', said Thomas as he knelt and worshipped.
After the resurrection appearances all doubt of Christ's divinity was
dispelled. Although Christian Jews still held to faith in the one
true God; it sometimes happened, as they knelt to pray, that the
face of Jesus appeared on the screen of their mind. Moreover,
after Pentecost, they had experienced in their lives the promised
Paraclete, the unseen Companion, Advocate, and Teacher. They
reverenced the indwelling Spirit of God who strengthened, inspired,
and encouraged them. They still prayed to the Heavenly Father, as
Jesus had taught them—and yet! and yet! they were discovering by
experience, more and more about God as Father, Son, and Holy
Spirit.

THE THREEFOLD BLESSING

It remains a mystery: but one thing is certain, that the doctrine
of the Trinity did not originate as a theory, but as a blessing.
It came out of the disciples' threefold experience of God in life
and worship. Christians used the trinitarian creed because without
it they could not express all that God had come to mean to them.
They could not tell of God in all his fulness without saying
'Father', 'Son', and 'Holy Spirit'. They worshipped the Divine
Father who had created them, the Divine Son who had redeemed
them, and God the Holy Spirit who sanctified them. They prayed
in the Triune Name; they preached in the Triune Name; and
they committed their souls to the Triune God who had blessed
them so signally. Dear to Christians are the words 'The grace
of our Lord Jesus Christ, and the love of God, and the fellowship of the Holy Spirit' (2 Corinthians 13.14 RSV). St Paul
used it to close his letters and invoke blessings on his friends.
He made it a gracious benediction upon the churches he had
started and served. Now we use it prayerfully for all who share

in the trinitarian faith. It completes every act of Christian worship. The Triune Name was said over us at baptism, and again at our confirmation, at our wedding; and when life closes, it will be used at our funeral to commit us to the eternal love of God.

It is the threefold cord that cannot be broken!

ST PETER'S DAY (29 June)
Quo Vadis?

I say unto thee, That thou art Peter, and upon this rock I will build my church . . . and I will give unto thee the keys of the kingdom of heaven.

MATTHEW 16.18,19

HIS NAME

When Simon first met Jesus, he was known as Simon, but Jesus said he would be called Cephas, translated Peter, the 'Rock'.

It was of course, more than a play on words. It was also a prediction, for at that moment Simon was anything but a rock, being as unstable as shifting sand. The Church of Rome has long made claim to Peter, resting its claim to authority on these words of Jesus. Yet, however the text is interpreted, it is clear that Jesus intended to make Peter, and the faith he had just confessed, the bedrock of the early Church. He became the spokesman of the Twelve, and was privileged to be one of the chosen three at the Transfiguration of Jesus, also in the Garden of Gethsemane. Peter was in fact given a position of pre-eminence in the early years of the Church; although in AD 49 St James became president of the church in Jerusalem, and Peter disappeared from the narrative of the Acts of the Apostles. Those who believe that he subsequently reappeared as Bishop of Rome, and was martyred there together with St Paul, rely for this conviction not on Scripture but on Church Tradition. However, St Peter is appointed a special day on which the Prayer Book commemorates the many excellent gifts Christ bestowed on him, and recalls his charge to become a faithful pastor of Christ's flock. Probably this is why Petertide is often chosen for ordinations into the sacred ministry of the Church.

The drama of his life and work is vividly presented in four scenes.

74

1. HIS CALL (by the lakeside)

To walk along the shores of Galilee is a magical experience. One is transported back in time to the New Testament days when Jesus walked by the same beach, saw the same sparkling waters, and the same encircling hills, dominated by snowy Mount Hermon in the distance. Here one can still see the fishermen casting circular hand-nets from the shore, or bigger nets from their boats. In imagination, one can also still see Peter and Andrew, James and John, washing their nets, with their boats just offshore. Nearby came a great crowd, pressing upon Jesus to hear the word of God. To get preaching-space, Jesus borrowed Peter's boat and asked him to thrust out a little from the land. Afterwards, Peter was told to launch out into the deep, where he was rewarded with a great shoal of fish. The miraculous catch filled him with awe and soul-searching. He fell down at Jesus' knees, saying 'depart from me, for I am a sinful man, O Lord' (Luke 5.8).

> Eternal Light! Eternal Light!
> How pure the soul must be,
> When, placed within Thy searching sight,
> It shrinks not, but, with calm delight,
> Can live, and look on Thee! (Thomas Binney)

The scene closes not with Christ forsaking Simon Peter, but calling him to become a follower. He was challenged to become a disciple, and with the call came the promise of yet bigger catches; not of fish but of men; to take them alive for the kingdom of heaven. He was given a glimpse of the far horizon, further then any yet seen on that inland lake.

> And Jesus said unto Simon, Fear not; from henceforth thou shalt catch men. And when they had brought their ships to land, they forsook all, and followed him. (Luke 5.10–11)

2. HIS CONFESSION (at the foot of Mount Hermon)

Twenty-five miles north of Lake Galilee is the poverty-stricken village of Banias, once the great city of Caesarea Philippi. Little remains of it now save the odd marble pillar seen by the wayside. Its attraction stems from the grandeur of the scene, and its association with Peter's great confession of faith in Jesus as the Christ. Here is the source of the river Jordan; and the site where Peter made the declaration of faith whence flows the faith of Christianity. Walking upstream one finds a great limestone cliff out of which pure water gushes; fed from the snowcaps of mighty Mount Hermon. This, too, is a place of magic! Here men have been moved to worship from time immemorial. It was one of the high places of the heathen god Baal. Carved in the cliff is a shrine and inscription to the Greek god Pan. But now the emperor after whom it was named is dead, and the ancient gods are dead; Christ, alone, lives for evermore!

> When Jesus came to the borders of Caesarea Philippi, he asked his disciples, saying, Whom do men say that I the Son of man am? ... And Simon Peter answered and said, Thou art the Christ, the Son of the living God. And Jesus answered and said unto him, Blessed art thou, Simon Bar-jona: for flesh and blood hath not revealed it unto thee, but my Father which is in heaven. And I say also unto thee, That thou art Peter, and upon this rock, I will build my church; and the gates of hell shall not prevail against it. (Matthew 16.13–18)

3. HIS DENIAL (in the courtyard of Caiaphas)

From the sunshine of Mount Hermon to the shadow of the cross was a long and painful pilgrimage. Yet, immediately after Peter's confession of faith, the disciples were forewarned that the Son of man must suffer.

> From that time forth began Jesus to show unto his disciples, how that he must go unto Jerusalem, and suffer many things of the elders and chief priests and scribes, and be killed ... (Matthew 16.21)

When Peter tried to dissuade him from that divinely-ordained path, he was sternly rebuked 'thou savourest not the things that be of God, but those that be of men'. It is of some comfort to us sinners, that even Peter was far from perfect. Although his warm, large-hearted, and outspoken personality made him an attractive leader; yet he shared our human weakness, and was at times both hot-headed and rashly impulsive with his promises. Until Jesus made

76

him a rock he could not be relied upon. During the years of his discipleship he had much to learn before he could become an apostle. It is sad to see him, after the arrest of Jesus, warming himself at the fire of Christ's enemies. It is even more sad to hear him in the courtyard of Caiaphas with cowardly oaths denying he ever knew Christ! When the cock crowed, Peter broke down and cried!

4. HIS RESTORATION (by the lake again)

When backsliding and despairing disciples long to find the place of renewal, they will find it where they first met with Jesus. Reading of Peter's restoration, I find myself carried back again to Peter's beloved lakeside. I see, as if it were but yesterday, a lovely garden by Lake Galilee. It is now called Tabghah (the place of seven springs), being the garden of a Christian hostel where are grown bananas, oranges, figs, and fruits of every kind. Here one may drink freely of the springs of pure, cool, refreshing water; or sit to meditate in the delightful grounds, where eucalyptus trees form an avenue down to the lakeside. This nearby shore, I feel sure, was the sacred place where Peter first heard the call of Christ, and where later he had his faith restored. Here, water from the springs of Tabghah runs down into the lake, attracting fish to the shallows where fishermen continue to cast hand-nets to enclose their catch, as described in the gospels. In the little chapel at Tabghah we were shown on the tessellated pavement an ancient representation of the loaves and fishes. I was fascinated, even more, by the huge stone used for a simple shrine by the shore. It was one of the great *Mensa Christi* stones, said to be used by the risen Christ for the sacred fire, on which bread and fish were laid at dawn for the returning disciples. Table of Christ stones! What a sacred table that proved! They ate in reverent silence 'knowing it was the Lord!' So when they had dined, Jesus said,

> Simon, son of Jonas, lovest thou me? . . . Feed my lambs. Simon, son of Jonas, lovest thou me? . . . Feed my sheep. Simon, son of Jonas, lovest thou me? . . . Feed my sheep. (John 21.15–16)

Three times Peter had denied, now Peter was given a threefold opportunity to reaffirm his love; and a lifetime to prove it by being a faithful pastor to Christ's flock.

Tradition says that when fierce persecution of the Christians started in Rome, Peter was urged to flee. Along the road as he fled, he met Christ his risen Lord, walking towards Rome. 'Quo vadis, Domine? (Where are you going, Lord?)'

'To Rome, to be crucified again for you!'

On hearing this, Peter went back to face martyrdom; and was crucified face downwards; as he felt unworthy to die in the same way as his Lord. What truth there is in this ancient story, I do not know; but I feel certain that Peter, after his threefold reaffirmation of love by the lakeside, never would again deny his Lord.

THE TRANSFIGURATION
The Glory of Christ

Jesus took Peter, James, and John his brother, and brought them unto a high mountain apart, and was transfigured before them: and his face did shine as the sun, and his raiment was white as the light.

MATTHEW 17.1–2

CHRIST CONFESSED

One of the most memorable experiences of a recent visit to the Holy Land was the journey to Banias, the biblical Caesarea Philippi, at the foot of Mount Hermon. I now think of those foothills as *the foothills of faith*; for it was there that Jesus drew out from Simon Peter the first great confession of faith: 'Thou art the Christ, the Son of the living God' (Matthew 16.16). It was also there that Jesus first began to speak about his approaching cross. Banias seems too pleasant a place to think of suffering and death. It is popular with hikers and holiday-makers, a place of mountain lakes and cooling streams, of rest and refreshment after the oppressive heat of the Jordan Valley. That may have been one of the reasons why Jesus took his disciples there, for they were tired and overwrought by the demands people had made on them in the previous months. In one day Jesus had dealt with the man torn by an unclean spirit, the woman tossing with fever in the house of Simon, and the diseased folk brought to his door at sunset. And so it had gone on, day after day, until the assisting disciples were in dire need of rest. So Jesus took them apart, to the hill-country to refresh their souls and strengthen their faith. As in Psalm 121, Jesus must often have lifted up his eyes unto the hills and their great Creator, from whence came his help. There they spent seven holy days (holi-days), and it was during this period when the three disciples had Jesus to themselves, that Simon came out with his clear declaration of faith 'Thou art the Christ, the Son of the living God' (Matthew 16.16). It marked out the first major milestone in Christian experience – the profession of personal faith in Jesus. There can be no further progress until that stage is reached. It needs to be clear, definite, and

79

personal. Others may have differing opinions of Jesus, but what matters is our own personal conviction. *'But whom do* you *say that I am?'*, asks Christ. He requires our personal response. We can make no further progress without a personal, individual, faith in Jesus as the Christ, God's anointed Saviour of men. It is the *sine qua non* of salvation. 'If thou shalt confess with thy mouth the Lord Jesus, and shalt believe in thine heart that God raised him from the dead, thou shalt be saved', said St Paul (Romans 10.9).

CHRIST WORSHIPPED

Once faith is confessed, there comes the urge and need to worship. We want to know more about Jesus, more of his saving power, more of his teaching, and more about his person. We need the further revelation that Jesus is not only the Saviour, but also the King to whom every knee must bow. So Jesus led them up a mountain to pray together. It is in the proximity of prayer, that we see him best. As Jesus prayed, to their amazed eyes he appeared in glorious majesty.

> The fashion of his countenance was altered, and his raiment became white and glistering. And, behold, there talked with him two men, which were Moses and Elias: Who appeared in glory, and spake of his decease [i.e., exodus, or deliverance] which he should accomplish at Jerusalem. (Luke 9.29–31; see also Mark 9 and Matthew 17)

Awestruck, they saw Jesus standing together with the great, with Moses and Elias, the great saints of the Old Testament. They felt on holy ground, that they should make tabernacles, take off their sandals, and worship. I think they would have wanted to sing

> Majesty, worship His Majesty;
> Unto Jesus be glory, honour, and praise.
> Majesty, kingdom authority,
> Flows from His throne unto His own,
> His Anthem raise. (J. W. Hatford)

Mount Hermon is majestic! Although Mount Tabor is the traditional site of the transfiguration, I believe that Mount Hermon, 9,000 feet above sea level, its snow slopes shining in the sun, to be

80

more likely than the rather ordinary-looking hill near Nazareth. No! I believe it was on the snow-slopes of Mount Hermon that the disciples saw Christ in shining splendour; his garments 'white and glistering', and his face glowing with the glory of God. What an inspiration to worship! It was as Isaiah promised: 'Thine eyes shall see the king in his beauty: they shall behold the land that is far off' (Isaiah 33.17).

Peter spoke for them all:

> Master, it is good for us to be here: let us make three tabernacles, one for thee, and one for Moses, and one for Elias . . . For he wist not what to say.

It was a vision they prayed would never fade. Here on this wonderful mountain they wished to stay, for ever and ever, amen. But they could no more stay on the mountain than we can stay in church! Religion must never become an escape from reality. Even on that wonderful mountain, shining in the sun, there came a cloud that overshadowed them; and they feared as they entered the cloud! The vision faded, Moses and Elias disappeared, and *They saw no man save Jesus only* (Mark 9.8). Thank God, Jesus stayed! He remains ever the same, 'yesterday, today, and for ever', constant in his compassion, beautiful in his purity, and majestic in his power. That part of the vision did not fade, they saw Jesus as King, and they could never forget. There came a time when they saw Jesus 'despised, and rejected of men', falsely accused, spat upon, robed in mock majesty, crowned with thorns, and crucified—but they never forgot his majesty on the Mount, and how they promised the allegiance of their lives.

CHRIST OBEYED

I wonder if you, too, have confessed faith in Christ, owned him as your King, and promised to follow him to the very end? How is it between you and Jesus *now*? Some delight to tell of their conversion, and confirmation, and the high peaks of their experience in the past; but where do they, and where do you, stand *now*? Has your vision been overshadowed by some cloud? Did something go dreadfully wrong with your faith, and did you stop following-on? It happens. In life we find sunshine and shadow, joy and sadness, faith and fear. Sometimes we feel on top of the world, at other times

81

we feel down. That's what happened to the disciples. Even while St Peter was making his plea to stay on the mountain, the clouds were gathering, the shadows darkening, and the vision fading. Soon could come the time when he must leave the bright mountain and go down into the dark valley to the vale of tears. In all the changing scenes of life, with its ups and downs, its mountains and valleys, its sunshine and shadows, there is one safeguard—keep close to Jesus. Follow him: Trust and obey him. Simon Peter wanted to stay on the mountain, but the Master called him to go down to the valley. Down there, were folk in dire need. Some were sick, and some were sad, and many were stricken with sin.

There was the broken-hearted father with his epileptic son. There, anxiously awaiting, were the rest of the disciples humiliated by their failure to help the lad, and surrounded by a jeering crowd. So down to the valley Jesus went, and called his disciples to follow. We must obey if our religion is to be real. Follow him! Religion that stays isolated on a mountain-top, or in a monastery remote from human need, is not the religion of Jesus. He goes where the need is greatest, and we must follow-on. Do you know the hymn *Follow On?*

> Down in the valley, or upon the mountain steep,
> Close beside my Saviour would my soul ever keep;
> He will lead me safely, in the path that He has trod,
> Up to where they gather on the hills of God.

And dare you sing the refrain?

> Follow! Follow! I would follow Jesus!
> Anywhere! everywhere, I would follow on!
> Follow! Follow! I would follow Jesus!
> Everywhere He leads me I would follow on! (R. Lowry)

Is that what you are doing *now*? Or are you stuck at some previous stage of your religious experience? You need to move on, in company with Christ from glory to glory advancing, to where the saints gather on the hills of God.

CHRIST EXPRESSED

Christ confessed, Christ worshipped, Christ followed—that's how Christian character is formed. The disciples kept close to Christ, and gradually they took on his characteristics. They became like him. People 'took knowledge of them, that they had been with Jesus' (Acts 4.13). The saints need no haloes, for goodness shows in their faces. They become Christ-like. It shows in their character and the beauty of their lives. They pray

> Let the beauty of Jesus be seen in me,
> All his wondrous compassion and purity.
> Oh, Thou Spirit Divine,
> All my nature refine,
> Till the beauty of Jesus be seen in me. (A. Orsborn)

Some would be embarrassed to be called a saint, but they have a saintliness of which they are unaware, a goodness of which they are not conscious shines out of their faces.

When Moses came down from the Holy Mount he was unaware that the goodness of God shone out of his face. So bright was 'the beauty of holiness' that sinners couldn't bear to look at his face. Yet, when he talked with Aaron, 'He wist not that the skin of his face shone'. Time spent with God produces a kind of spiritual induction. Place an iron rod close to a powerful magnet, and in time it will become magnetic. Leave it in a hot fire, and it will glow. Live close to Christ, day by day, and you will take on Christian characteristics. In time you will bear his likeness. St Paul spoke of living 'in Christ'; and it transformed him. From his experience as an evangelist he knew that even the most evil-faced of men could be converted, changed, and brought to bear the likeness of Christ. Writing to converts from the foul community of Corinth he said

> But we *all*, with open face beholding as in a glass the glory of the Lord, are changed into the same image from glory to glory, even as by the Spirit of the Lord. (2 Corinthians 3.18)

That is the secret—beholding! Beholding Christ day by day changes us. Living close to Jesus transforms us. There is a process of spiritual transfiguration. Others will see it in our faces, and it will be expressed unconsciously in all we do or say. Read and re-read the gospels, picture Christ in all his ways, pray and meditate upon his words. It is like seeing him 'as in a glass', not only a mirror to reflect his image, but also a telescope to bring him near. Thus beholding, the Spirit of Christ will work in us, until one day, please God, 'We shall be like him; for we shall see him as he is' (1 John 3.2).

Not only in the words you say
  Not only in your deeds confessed,
But in a most unconscious way
  Is Christ expressed.
Is it a beatific smile?
  A holy light upon your brow?
Oh No! I felt His presence while
  You laughed, just now.
To me, 'twas not the truths you taught
  To you so clear, to me still dim,
But when you came to us you brought
  A sense of Him.
And from your eyes He beckons me
  And from your lips His love is shed,
Till I lose sight of you,
  And see the Christ, instead. (Anon)

ST MATTHEW'S DAY (21 September)
God, or Mammon

Jesus ... saw a publican, named Levi, sitting at the receipt of custom: and he said unto him, Follow me. And he left all, rose up, and followed him.

LUKE 5.27–28

HIS DESPICABLE TRADE

I have always thought it unfair that perfectly decent innkeepers should be called 'publicans', for the *publicani* of New Testament times were a thoroughly disreputable lot of traitors to their fellow-countrymen, having agreed to extort taxes on behalf of the foreign occupation force. These minor officials of puppet King Herod were unscrupulous quislings, and merciless in the way they carried on their terrible trade of extortion; usually taking far more than was due, in order to line their own pockets. They were men of greed who had made mammon their God, and were known as 'publicans and sinners'. Matthew was such a man!

> A man of scorned and hardening trade,
> alike the symbol and the tool
> of foreign master's hated rule.

Lust for money breeds a host of evils. Day by day, Matthew shut his ears to the cries of the poor and oppressed. He hardened his heart and ignored his conscience. Every night he entered up the day's takings, and gloated over his cashbook as materially he grew richer and richer, whilst impoverishing his soul. It is said that the love of money is the root of all evil, and so it proved with Matthew. One thing led to another. He had already sold his country, and his spiritual birthright; and now he was about to sell his soul. He had forfeited the respect of family and friends, as daily he became more and more corrupt. So far had he been swept along by his lust for money that, had he not responded to the call of Christ that day, he might have been lost for ever. Below the mighty Niagara Falls the river narrows and the current quickens, becoming ever more

85

powerful and perilous. Canoeists can be rescued from the rapids until 'redemption point' is passed. Matthew was rapidly nearing that point! Thank God he left that perilous customs-post when he did.

During our visit to Israel, we were walking along the shores of Galilee when we came across some huge hewn stones which served as a surprising reminder of this story. According to H.V. Morton, they may have come from the ancient quayside of Capernaum. They were heart-shaped, with a worn hole in the centre made by the ring-bolts of the fishermen. It was on this quay that Matthew probably had his customs-hut, to collect tax on fish or goods unloaded by the boatmen.

HIS TROUBLED CONSCIENCE

The gospels are, of course, compressed accounts. A superficial reading of Matthew's conversion might lead one to suppose that on the spur of the moment the tax collector deserted his post at the call, without previous knowledge of Jesus or any lead-up to that life-changing decision. More careful consideration, however, must lead to the conclusion that from his customs-post Matthew must often have seen Jesus in Capernaum, and even heard his preaching in the open air. Had he heard the parable of the talents? And the story of the man without mercy, who took his fellow-servant by the throat, and cast him into prison for the sake of a hundred pence? Had he heard Jesus talk about the impossibility of serving God and mammon? Did he know the proverb about the camel and the eye of a needle; and the sheer impossibility of entering heaven by those who are 'loaded'? Did it make Matthew squirm to hear about the wealthy farmer who planned ease in his retirement, but forgot about his soul? I believe these things pricked the conscience of Matthew, and started a struggle in his soul that could not be resolved without a radical change of life. Despite the dirty work he did for the Romans, he was still a Jew, brought up to believe in the sovereignty and justice of God. Though too ashamed to attend the local synagogue, and shunned by the more righteous folk who did; yet, religious belief was not yet dead in him. He was torn between the desire to get right with God and the desire to keep his ill-gotten riches. As the hymn puts it, he was 'tossed about with many a conflict, many a doubt, fighting and fears within, without'. There is no torture like the self-torture of indecision;

especially if the choice is between right and wrong. It might well have led to a total mental and moral breakdown, had not Christ called him in time.

HIS CHRISTIAN CONVERSION

I don't suppose that when Matthew went to the office that fateful day he had any idea that it would be for the last time. He tidied his desk, propped open the door, and sat waiting to catch the first customer. Little did he imagine that it would be Christ, and that *he* would make the demand. Through the open door Jesus saw him sitting at the seat of custom. He saw the cash-book and the records of extortion, and looked straight into the eyes of Matthew, filled with guilt and shame. He saw the inner conflict, the struggle between right and wrong, and that the crisis had come. It was not a moment to mince words. 'Follow me!' Jesus called. It was the divine demand that may not be denied. And Matthew left all, rose up, and followed him (see Matthew 9.9).

His conversion was as sudden, decisive, and complete as that! He left the ledger and all the tools of extortion on the desk, slammed the office door, and went out to become a follower of Christ. Let us not complicate the meaning of conversion, or disguise what is involved. It is a turning, a complete about-turn, an utter change of attitude to Christ and the way we live. For Matthew it was a resolve to obey, and a movement of faith that involved all that he was, and all he had. He left all, rose up, and stepped out. It reminds us of Billy Graham's evangelistic call 'to get right up out of your seat'. The response to Christ involves every part of us, our body as well as our mind. It is not just emotional. It demands a radical rethink about our way of life, and an act of will in resolving to change. Matthew couldn't be converted in his mind, and then remain sitting there, to let things go as before. The present and future were called into question as well as the past. Life can never be the same when we respond to the call of Christ.

HIS COMPLETE CHANGE

(a) *His changed name*
Everything changed for Matthew, even his name. He used to be

called 'Levi the publican', or names even worse! He had a name for meanness, money-grabbing, and callousness to others in distress; but not now. His Christian friends began to call him Matthew, which means 'gift of God'. His name changed along with his change of character. Just as Simon became Peter, and Saul became Paul, so did 'Levi the publican' eventually become *Saint* Matthew. He renounced the hidden things of dishonesty, no longer walking in craftiness, but walking after Christ. Gradually, he became like the One he followed. Conversion changes character.

(b) *His changed concern*

Before conversion Matthew's chief concern was for money. He lived for it. It motivated his day to day existence. For it, he sacrificed his friends, his self-respect, his country, and his religion. Money became his God, but not now! After conversion, he became concerned about the condition and fate of his fellow sinners. He had found Christ and an infinitely better way of life, and he wanted them to find it, too. So, surprisingly, and uncharacteristically, he spent a lot of money and 'made him a great feast in his own house' (Luke 5.29). 'Him' I think *should* have a capital H. The feast was for Jesus. It was to provide an opportunity for Jesus to meet other publicans and sinners, and do the same for them. 'And there was a great company of publicans and of others.' The new Matthew had a great concern for others and for their salvation. The publican had become an evangelist.

(c) *His changed occupation*

It was not that the publican turned preacher. There is no mention in the New Testament of Matthew preaching like Peter or Paul. Preaching was not his forte, but he had other talents. He was good at making notes, and accurate in book-keeping; but lacked ability to speak in public. According to an early historian (Eusebius) he once tried to preach; but then trusted his pen rather than his tongue to do the work of evangelism. When he moved on, he left behind notes for the gospel that bears his name. He may not have had a gift for preaching, but he was a ready writer. His pen was the one thing he didn't leave behind in the tax office. He put it to good use, taking notes of the Sermon on the Mount and other sayings of Jesus. They provided the material for the Gospel according to St Matthew. Pictures of him in stained-glass windows showing him holding the money-bag are mistaken. When Christ

called, he finished with money-bags for ever – that job fell to Judas
Iscariot!

The Collect for St Matthew's day

O Almighty God, who by thy blessed Son didst call Matthew
from the receipt of custom to be an Apostle and Evangelist:
Grant us grace to forsake all covetous desires, and inordinate
love of riches, and to follow the same thy Son Jesus Christ, who
liveth and reigneth with Thee and the Holy Ghost, one God,
world without end. Amen. (Book of Common Prayer)

MICHAELMAS
I Believe in Angels

STORIES OF ANGELS

Forty or more years ago, I was one of a group of hopeful young men in St Paul's Cathedral, London, about to be ordained into the sacred ministry of the Church, commissioned to preach the everlasting Gospel of Christ. The years of preparation were over, the legal requirements had been met; soon we would make our vows, and the hands of all the bishops present would be laid upon us to convey both authority and blessing. Thus commissioned, we waited eagerly for the ordination sermon, to be delivered by one of the senior clergy. It was moment of great expectancy as he gave out the text; for was not this Michaelmas, the day of St Michael and All Angels? We, too, were now ready to go forth and do battle with the dragons of evil and the monsters that menace mankind. The angels were on our side. Imagine, therefore, our deflation, when the preacher pricked our hopes with a pin! He began with the silly story of mediaeval theologians debating how many angels could dance on the head of a pin. I've forgotten the rest of the sermon, but I sadly remember that one of the young men hid his clerical collar as he left the church!

FANCIFUL PICTURES OF ANGELS

In fairness to the preacher, I am sure that he must have had many good things to follow, had we continued to listen; for the Michaelmas message contains much to challenge and encourage the disciples of Jesus. Why, then, are folk so ready to dismiss the idea of angels, as we dismiss stories of fairies down the garden, or pixies in the wood? Is it because of fairy-tales, and fanciful pictures of angels with wings in children's books?

Some stained-glass windows show St Michael as a winged knight in shining armour, with drawn sword, and his foot on a dragon. Is

it because of these fanciful images that folk find it hard to believe
in the mighty angels of biblical record? 'I believe in angels!' sings
a sentimental pop star; so do I, but not in any soft and sentimental way. I believe in them as they appear in Scripture, and
are experienced in real life.

THE BIBLE AND THE ANGELS

So who are the angels? What are they like, and what purpose do
they serve? What says the Word of God? The Bible speaks of angels
being the messengers of God, sent forth to convey his messages to
human beings. Sometimes they appear in human form, as when two
men were sent to inform Abraham of the child of promise. Human-
like messengers at which Sarah dared to laugh! Sometimes they
appeared as supernatural beings, as in Isaiah's awesome vision of
the six-winged seraphim crying 'Holy, Holy, Holy'. But, whether
in human or supernatural form, winged or not, the mighty messengers of God inspire awe; for they are 'all ministering spirits,
sent forth to minister for them who shall be heirs of salvation'
(Hebrews 1.4).

How then do they minister to mankind? No human being in his
normal conscious state is recorded as ever having seen a winged
angel. They have been seen in trance, or dream, but not by men
awake. Jacob dreamed of angels, ascending and descending on the
ladder set up between earth and heaven; but when he awoke they
had vanished. Later, however, at the brook Jabbok, 'there wrestled
a *man* with him until the breaking of the day' (Genesis 32.24). The
angel was in human form, but Jacob was in no doubt that he had
met with an agent of God. Awestruck, he renamed that place Peniel,
'the face of God' (Genesis 32.30).

JESUS AND THE ANGELS

In whatever form the angel Gabriel appeared to Mary at the annun-
ciation, it is evident that the vision produced in her reverent
submission to the will of God. When the birth of Jesus was
made known to the shepherds, the angel appeared supernaturally
in a blaze of glory, and the heavens resounded with the song of the

angelic host. In Christ's ordeal of the wilderness temptations and at Gethsemane we are told that angels came to comfort him. They were very real to him. He believed in their power to help, and that had he called – 'more than twelve legions of angels' would have come to rescue him from the cross (Matthew 26.53). The resurrection was made known by a vision of angels, in what form we do not know, save that St Mark tells us they saw 'a young man sitting on the right side [of the sepulchre] clothed in a long white garment; and they were afraid' (Mark 16.5). However, Jesus said little about the angels in his teaching, except for a few scattered references. He said children must not be despised for 'in heaven their angels do always behold the face of my Father which is in heaven' (Matthew 18.10). Asked about the married state and the after-life, he replied 'In the resurrection they neither marry, nor are given in marriage, but are as the angels of God in heaven' (Matthew 22.30). Concerning repentant sinners, he said 'There is joy in the presence of the angels of God over one sinner that repenteth' (Luke 15.7). Finally, he said that at his second coming he would return in the glory of his Father with the holy angels (Mark 8.38).

THE APOSTLES AND THE ANGELS

The Acts of the Apostles tells of angels accomplishing their deliverance from prison: 'the angel of the Lord opened the prison doors, and brought them forth' (Acts 5.19). St Peter was guided to minister to Cornelius and the Gentiles by a vision brought by an angel (Acts 10.3). St Paul was strengthened in the storm by the vision of an angel: 'there stood by me this night the angel of God, whose I am, and whom I serve, Saying, Fear not, Paul . . .' (Acts 27.23–24). Evidently, both to Christ, and to his apostles, the ministry of angels was very real, in whatever form they appeared. Heaven they believed to be populated by 'an innumerable company of angels' (Hebrews 12.22), although on earth they appeared in numerous guises, often in human form. Just as the risen Christ appeared to Mary in the guise of a Gardener, and to the disciples of Emmaus as a Stranger on the road, so they were exhorted 'Be not forgetful to entertain strangers; for thereby some have entertained angels unawares' (Hebrews 13.2).

ST MICHAEL AND ALL ANGELS

Which brings us to St Michael, the beloved patron of many churches dedicated in his name. In the Book of Revelation he appears as head of the angelic host, going forth to do victorious battle with the forces of evil:

> And the great dragon was cast out, that old serpent, called the Devil, and Satan, which deceiveth the whole world. (Revelation 12.9)

The Dragon's greatest deception was to persuade people that he, Satan, did not really exist, that goodness and evil were not real issues, and that angels of God were merely the fantasies of weak minds. The Church of God, however, was not deceived. It perceived the moral issues, recognized the nature of evil, and fought to uphold God's standard of righteousness. That is why St Michael and All Angels is one of the major religious festivals on which men are ordained into the sacred ministry, and why on that day we pray

> O Everlasting God, who hast ordained and constituted the services of Angels and men in a wonderful order: Mercifully grant, that as thy holy Angels always do thee service in heaven, so by thy appointment they may succour and defend us on earth; through Jesus Christ our Lord. (Book of Common Prayer)

HARVEST TIME
God's Ingathering

A time to plant and a time to pluck up.

ECCLESIASTES 3.2

Harvest time crowns the year. The hard work of ploughing, sowing, and tending is finally crowned with the fruits of man's labour. All he asks now is a few weeks of good reaping weather, to gather in the golden grain and the fruit. What was sown in hope and tended in faith, is reaped in joy. When all is safely gathered-in, the celebrations of Harvest Home begin. The village church is decorated with fruit and flowers and vegetables, and well attended for the traditional service of Harvest Thanksgiving. Even the town folk find that the festival remains one of the most popular services of the year, and they love to sing the hymns and rejoice in God's goodness. They give thanks that again God has honoured the ancient promise,

> While the earth remaineth, seedtime and harvest, and cold and heat, and summer and winter, and day and night shall not cease. (Genesis 8.22)

Of course, there is more to the Harvest Festival than hymns and thanksgiving for *material* blessings. Jesus loved to speak of the flowers of the field, of the time of sowing and reaping, of wheat and tares, and the need for good grain. He told parables of ploughing, harvesting, and the man who needed bigger barns. In his teaching Jesus was very down to earth, but he lifted men's thoughts heavenwards. When the Samaritans flocked out of the city to see him, he said they were 'white unto harvest'—a harvest of souls. When a few Greeks desired to see him, Jesus saw them as the first fruits of a great ingathering of the Gentiles. Of his approaching cross he said—'Except a corn of wheat fall into the ground, and die, it abideth alone: but if it die, it bringeth forth much fruit' (John 12.24). Jesus spoke of the fields, and the acres of ripening corn; but saw them as signs of a yet more wonderful world. He made of earthly things parables of heaven.

He spoke of grass, and wind, and rain, and fig-trees and fair
    weather;
And made it His delight to bring Heaven and earth together.
(T. T. Lynch)

THE SCENE

Picture in imagination the scene on the day Jesus preached the
parable of the sower. The setting of his sermon was on the
northern shore of the Sea of Galilee, where a semi-circular cove
forms a kind of open-air theatre. 'Behold!' he shouted, and pointed
across to the hillside where a farmer was sowing seed. He wanted
people not just to hear, but to *see* the truth proclaimed. He wanted
them to see the spiritual significance of that familiar scene, and to
ponder its meaning for their lives. What they looked on was not a
neatly fenced field of the English countryside, but the rugged landscape of Galilee. The ground was rough and stony, crossed by a
well-worn footpath, baked hard by the Eastern sun. Here and there,
thorn bushes and weeds had taken root among the rocks, making
it hard going for the ploughman, and chancy soil for the sower.
Above, waited the birds, about to snatch away the surface laid seed.

THE SEED

Look then first at the seed. We cannot misunderstand what it represents, for Jesus himself explained. He provided his own interpreta-
tion of the parable. 'The seed', he said, 'is the word of God.' It is
good seed. It is the good news of the kingdom of God. It is the
Gospel. It may seem tiny, but it will grow. It holds great potential.
In it lies hope for the souls of men, for it is the seed-corn of
salvation.

When the Pilgrim Fathers set off in the *Mayflower* to seek a better
life in the New World, they loaded axes to fell trees and build log
cabins, tools to till the ground; and what they hoped would be
sufficient food to see them through the dreaded winter, until the
first harvest. Carefully loaded were the sacks of precious seed-corn,
on which they relied for that vital harvest. Therein lay their hope
of salvation from starvation. Any good American can tell the
gruesome story of that awful winter when his ancestors nearly

starved to death. It is remembered at every Thanksgiving. They recall how the pilgrim pioneers tried to exist on wild berries when the food stocks were finished; and how hard it was for the Pilgrim Fathers to resist the temptation to eat the seed-corn. Year by year, the story is repeated of the hopes and fears and desperate prayers of the pioneer families. The seed-corn saved, and then sowed, produced their salvation. Without that first anxiously-awaited crop the Pilgrims would have perished. Perhaps Jeremiah had something like this in mind when he cried 'The harvest is past, the summer is ended, and we are not saved' (Jeremiah 8.20).

And yet, said Jesus, 'Man shall not live by bread alone, but by every word that proceedeth out of the mouth of God' (Matthew 4.4).

The word of God is the seed-corn of the soul.

THE SOWER

So much for the seed: now see the sower! Who scatters the seed of the soul? There can be little doubt that Jesus saw himself as the sower. The parable was a bit of biography. It laid out his life's work, the meaning of his mission, and the purpose of his preaching. By preaching and teaching he, the Heavenly Sower, scattered precious seed. Like the earthly sower, he had tilled hard soil, for the souls of many were hard and unreceptive. He had worked among those whom sin had hardened – the publicans, and the prostitutes, and the self-righteous. Sinners were hard soil, but he had sowed in hope. The Gospel had been preached with great grace, and without discrimination to all men everywhere. He had harrowed a hard furrow, and trodden a painful path on rocky ground. He had prayed and suffered for the souls of men, in hope of reaping. The harvest hymn says

> Behold the Heavenly Sower
>   goes forth with better seed
> The word of sure salvation
>   with hands and feet that bleed.

THE SOIL

So much for the Seed and the Sower, but what of the Soil? Ah! said Jesus, the soil is the heart or soul of the hearer, his very self. Some, said Jesus, are like the wayside, like that hard-beaten path across the field. *Their hearts are hard,* resistant to receiving the Word. Sinning hardens the soul; and with hardened sinners the sower seems to work in vain. All the harrowing and sowing seems wasted, for they remain indifferent to the Gospel. Spiritual sclerosis has set in the soul. Habit has thickened the sinners' skin. The Gospel is rejected; and soon Satan snatches away the seed 'lest they should believe and be saved' (Luke 8.12; see also Matthew 13 and Mark 4).

And there are *shallow hearts,* said Jesus, folk who are superficial, people with no depth. They are like the stony places 'because they had no deepness of earth . . . and because they had no root, they withered away'. They are rootless, for they seldom pray, or read, or meditate upon the things of God. Their life is lived at a shallow level. They are emotional, easily swayed, quickly converted, and as quickly turned back. 'These receive the word with joy; but have no root, which for a while believe, but in time of testing fall away.'

And *hearts that are choked,* said Jesus. People's lives are cluttered with all kinds of things, and seed sown in their hearts becomes choked. Usually they are busy people — too busy with the wrong things. Their constant excuse for neglecting things more worthy is 'I've no time'. Prayer is crowded out, Bible reading neglected, churchgoing displaced by other activities. Their hearts, said Jesus, become choked 'with the cares and riches of *this* life; and bring no fruit to perfection'. They have

> Room for pleasure, room for business;
>   but for Christ the crucified
> Not a place that He can enter
>   in the heart for which he died.

How well the Heavenly Sower understands the souls of men! 'He knew what was in man', said his disciples. He reads their hearts and explores the deepest recesses of their being. He knows the hard-hearted, the superficial, and worldly-minded. He knows how unreceptive some of us seem; and yet, with amazing grace, he goes on sowing his word and offering the Gospel, in hope of our responding. He knows some soil is poor; but knows, too, that the seed of the Gospel is good. It holds tremendous potential for our lives.

Lastly, said Jesus, there are not only hard hearts and shallow hearts and choked hearts; but also *good hearts,* hearts receptive of

97

the good seed, of the Word of God. 'These are they which in an honest and good heart, having heard the word, keep it, and bring forth fruit with patience.'

Many years ago, farmers trying to scrape a living from the dusty plains of Ontario despaired of their seeds ever taking root before the fierce winds swept them away. But a man named Marquis decided to develop an experimental seed, tough enough to survive even the fiercest wind. After many failures, he finally produced a small sack of his own brand of stronger seed. He took it before the Agricultural Board, but his claims were dismissed. So Marquis went away, and waited until one of the remaining farmers had tried again to produce a crop. Then secretly, Marquis sowed his own seed over the same ground. Months later, he took an aerial photograph, and there plainly written by rich luxuriant growth among the thin stalks was the word 'MARQUIS'! It is now recognized as good strong seed, and is the standard seed used in Ontario.

The Gospel, said Jesus, is *good* seed, and, sown in honest hearts, will produce thirty, sixty, a hundred-fold! So what sort of soil are *we*?

> Here in his church 'tis scattered,
>   our spirits are the soil:
> Then let an ample fruitage
>   repay His pain and toil.
>   (W. St Hill Bourne)

ST LUKE'S DAY (18 October)
Hospital Sunday

Luke, the beloved physician . . . sends greetings.

COLOSSIANS 4.14

The Patron Saint of the medical profession sends greetings to all who on this Hospital Sunday share his compassion and desire to heal the sick. Jesus, himself, was known as the Great Physician, and such was his reputation as a healer, that men said of him 'He hath done all things well: he maketh both the deaf to hear and the dumb to speak' (Mark 7.37).

A FIGURE OF FUN

Not every kind of illness or disability excites compassion. The man they nicknamed Mogilalos was treated by the unkind as a figure of fun. He was a deaf-mute. The gospel says he 'had an impediment in his speech'. Being unable to hear his own voice, he couldn't correct his pronunciation, and uttered uncouth noises whenever he tried to speak. They called him Mogilalos, for that's how it sounded when he babbled and spluttered. Understandably, he retreated into the silence shared with the dumb. He became both deaf *and* dumb!

It makes me admire all the more the courage of those who try to cope despite their double handicap. I know a missionary who contracted middle-ear disease in Iran, which left him both hard-of-hearing and strangely spoken. Withdrawn from service abroad, he decided to serve the Church at home; where he took up the challenge of a church so poorly-attended that it was in danger of closure. His voice had an odd metallic tone, which made him a poor preacher. Yet he proved so good a pastor, and so assiduous in visiting his parishioners, that by faith and friendship he filled the church. Thank God for friendship! Mogilalos had a few good friends, who cared enough to bring him to Jesus, and to the finest Friend of all.

99

A FRIEND IN NEED

There before Jesus stood poor Mogilalos—deaf, dumb, and ridiculous. The crowd laughed, but not Jesus! When they 'besought Jesus to lay his hand upon him', the Saviour was so stirred that a sigh of compassion came up from the depths of his soul.

I wonder how many people feel a like compassion and whether, like the friends of Mogilalos, they beseech Jesus in prayer for the sick? They brought the deaf-mute to Jesus, and besought him for their afflicted friend. Surely this should be the practical outcome of professed faith and concern for others? For what other purpose is the Decade of Evangelism? And what is evangelism but bringing men to Jesus? Somehow, these friends of Mogilalos had found faith. Perhaps they had heard of Jesus taking by the hand Simon's wife's mother who lay sick of a fever, and how she had been healed. Or perhaps they had heard of how Jesus stretched forth his hand to touch and cleanse the leper. Now they wanted Jesus to take poor Mogilalos in hand. They besought him to heal, and Jesus responded in a way that was both compassionate and complete. Personal problems need private attention. So the first essential for Mogilalos was to get him away from the crowd, for men's mockery would quickly reduce him to hopeless confusion. 'And Jesus took him aside from the multitude' (Mark 7.33).

Christ's way of dealing with people in distress merits close attention by members of the medical profession.

1. When healing Mogilalos, Jesus showed *great sensitivity*.
He sensed what mockery would do to Mogilalos, and realized his need for a private interview. Although Christ was concerned for the multitudes, and spoke of them as sheep without a shepherd, yet he dealt with them as individuals, each was precious in his sight. Like a good shepherd he knows each one of us by name, and deals with us individually. As in the parable of the the ninety-nine sheep, he searches out the one that is lost, binds up its wounds and brings it back to the fold. Mass evangelism may have its merits, but salvation is always personal. Wherever one meets with Christ, whether in a public gathering, or in private prayer, the contact is always personal. Some encounter Christ in the congregation, others in solitude; but each is dealt with individually. We each have a different need, which Christ meets in a special way. He is sensitive to our needs. Mogilalos needed a private interview, so Jesus 'took him aside from the multitude'.

2. Secondly, notice that Christ communicated with *great simplicity*. With Mogilalos there was the great problem of communication. The barrier of deafness isolated him. His uncouth speech cut him off from his fellows. He had double trouble, and needed Christ's double cure – don't we all? The hymn voices our need: 'Be of sin the double cure, cleanse me from its guilt and power.' Specially trained clergy skilled in difficult deaf-and-dumb language are needed to communicate with the afflicted; but Jesus made Mogilalos understand with the simplest of signs. 'And Jesus put his fingers into his ears, and he spat, and touched his tongue' (Mark 7.33). What could be more simple to understand, or more powerful to receive, than the healing touch of Jesus in the place where it matters most?

3. Thirdly, we see Christ's *great sympathy*.

'And looking up to heaven, he sighed.' Looking on poor Mogilalos, standing there before him shamefaced with all the misery of a misfit, Jesus was stirred to the depths of his being. He was truly 'the man of sorrows and acquainted with grief', and he groaned with a grief too agonizing for words. Have you ever felt such sympathy for others? How deep goes your compassion? Does it go deeper than words? From Jesus a grief-stricken plea went straight to heaven. 'Surely', said the prophet, 'He hath borne our griefs, and carried our sorrows' (Isaiah 53.4). His heaven-sent sigh came from a sympathy too deep for words. It was sent to heaven, for there is no place where earth's sorrows are more deeply felt. 'God so loved . . .' Soon Jesus, himself, would personally feel what it was like to be mocked and set at nought, to stand in silence while fools had their fun at his expense. It was fellow-feeling that sent up a human groan to the heavenly Father's breast. 'And looking up to heaven, he sighed, and saith unto him Ephphatha, that is, Be opened' (Mark 7.34).

How strange that the actual word Jesus used has been kept for centuries in the original Aramaic tongue! The gospels have been translated into a thousand different tongues, yet the actual word the Saviour said to Mogilalos has been preserved intact. Did the healed man keep repeating it – 'Ephphatha! Ephphatha, Ephphatha'? And was it 'music in the sinner's ear' too precious to lose? The first sound Mogilalos had ever heard was the Saviour's voice, and it sounded the 'open sesame' of his soul. It opened up for him a whole new life. Gone were the uncouth years, the mockery, and the isolation he had so long endured. Christ, the Son of God had spoken, and his life was transformed.

101

4. Fourthly, note Christ's thoroughness – *the cure was made complete*.

Christ never leaves his work half-done. He not only opened the man's ears, but also loosened his tongue. He satisfies those who seek his help – completely! 'And straightaway his ears were opened, *and* the string of his tongue was loosed, and he spake plain' (Mark 7.35)!

His deafness was cured, and so was his dumbness. The man spake plainly. There was no more mumbling, but speech that was clear and well-expressed. The astonished crowd testified 'He hath done all things *well*: he maketh the deaf to hear, *and* the dumb to speak'.

CHRIST IN THE PRESENT

The healing work of Christ should never be relegated to the past, for the Greek New Testament uses the present continuous tense for the healing ministry of Christ: *'He goes on doing* all things well.' Christ's blessed ministry did not cease at the cross, or at the close of the New Testament. It still goes on! His touch has *still* its ancient power. No word from him can fruitless fall. Christ never will leave his work half-done. His is a continuing ministry of wholeness. He knows no half-measures. His intention is not to open our ears to the word of salvation, and then leave us too tongue-tied to tell others. The Good News must spread. You and I, no less than dear old Mogilalos, have a Gospel to tell, and a witness to give. Well did Charles Wesley long for a thousand tongues to sing his dear Redeemer's praise:

> Hear him, ye deaf; his praise, ye dumb,
> Your loosened tongues employ;
> Ye blind, behold your Saviour come;
> And leap, ye lame, for joy!

ALL SAINTS' DAY
Never Alone

Wherefore, seeing we also are compassed about with so great a cloud of witnesses, let us lay aside every weight, and the sin which doth so easily beset us, and let us run with patience the race that is set before us.

HEBREWS 12.1

THE SAINTS LOOK ON

Few of us will forget the Olympic Games held in Barcelona, and the vast crowd of spectators in the magnificent stadium. It reminded me of the ancient stadia in Greece, and the impressive amphitheatres with seats rising tier upon tier almost to the sky. I pictured the sport contests of old, with races, and wrestling bouts, and gladiators fighting for their very lives; cheered on by the watching crowd. Was this in the mind of the writer of the Epistle to the Hebrews when he described 'a great cloud of witnesses'? He uses a Greek word for 'witnesses' (*marturōn*) to suggest that those who looked on were the saints who had made a brave witness for Christ and the Gospel. They were the martyrs, who in their day had 'run the straight race through God's good grace', and 'fought the good fight with all their might'. They were the veteran saints, who had 'resisted unto blood' every attempt to make them give up their Christian testimony.

We, too, as Christians, have a race to be run, and a fight to be won; and to know that the victors of previous contests surround us gives great encouragement. The heroes of faith in Old Testament days are listed in the eleventh chapter of the Epistle to the Hebrews. They are described as men and women 'of whom the world was not worthy'. The list is long, but many more could be added to the roll of honour. I am thinking of the New Testament saints and martyrs, and the brave witnesses in the following centuries: Polycarp, the aged Bishop of Smyrna, 'firm as an anvil when it is smitten'; and John Bunyan, in the Bedford gaol; and Bishop Hannington, and James Chalmers, and other missionary martyrs. Among the 'cloud of witnesses' must surely be seen the Wesley brothers, and Fletcher,

103

the saintly Vicar of Madeley; and Henry Martyn, the missionary scholar of India and Persia; and self-sacrificing Hudson Taylor of the China Inland Mission; and many more recent saints. The list seems endless as we recall the faces of those we have 'loved long since, and lost awhile'; for they, too, are part of the great cloud of witnesses which cheers us on our way.

> For all the saints who from their labours rest,
> Who Thee by faith before the world confessed,
> Thy name, O Jesus, be for ever blest. Alleluia!

THE STRUGGLE GOES ON

The French language makes a clear distinction between those who say they 'go in for sport', and those who actively participate. Compare those watching from a comfortable armchair a football match on the television screen, with the football-team straining every sinew to score. Whatever the spectators have paid to watch is trivial, compared with what it costs the players. I think 'players' is a misnomer, for the teams in serious matches don't play, but fight to the finish; and the same might be said of the Olympic Games and athletic contests. Those who have actively participated in the contests of former years understand what it takes in terms of tough training and unsparing effort to win. As they witness the athletes straining every nerve and ounce of strength to win, the cloud of witnesses is anything but passive. They are emotionally involved, willing then to win, and cheering them on.

So, too, in the Christian arena; everyone is involved. There are no passengers, or impassive lookers-on. The Church militant is urged on by the Church triumphant (those whose race is done and whose fight is won). The encouraging cheers are the shouts of the saints, apostles, and martyrs. The Church on earth receives encouragement from the Church in heaven. The support comes from the great Communion of Saints, the vast multitude which no man can number. Some years ago an attempt was made to count the number of Christians, country by country, throughout the world. According to statistics then available the approximate number was 800 million! But even that immense number accounts for but a small part of the whole church. The universal Church of Christ consists of the whole company of believers, in all times and ages, in heaven and on earth. To count the Communion of Saints you would have to go back through the centuries, detail the present, and then stretch forward into the unknown future. It is an innumerable number, of the living, the so-called 'dead', and those yet to be born. It includes the Church triumphant in heaven, as well as the Church militant here on earth. In spiritual terms, the Church is nothing less than the Body of Christ; and therefore cannot be treated in human terms, nor counted as one might count the membership of some secular association. The Communion of Saints is a countless host, that great multitude which no man can number.

> From earth's wide bounds, from ocean's farthest coast,
> Through gates of pearl streams in the countless host,
> Singing to Father, Son, and Holy Ghost. Alleluia!

THE FAITHFUL PRESS ON

'You'll never walk alone!' is the popular song of the Liverpool football supporters. It moves the emotions of the fans, but there is a wider and deeper implication for the faithful.

Some years ago I talked with a fine young fellow who had just accepted a missionary call to serve a widely scattered pastorate somewhere within the Arctic Circle. Whenever I have prayed for him, I've tried to imagine the hardships such sacrificial service involves. I think of the great loneliness he must feel as he travels across the icy wastes of his vast parish, to reach the remote homes and hearts of the Eskimo people. I wonder if, sometimes, he feels 'one on his own', chilled and discouraged by hearts as hard as the ice. Or does he feel his heart strangely warmed, realizing 'He'll never walk alone'? It is one thing to bawl those words in a football crowd, but another to sing them in the lonely Arctic wastes! I like to believe that as he plods along the trail previous missionaries have pioneered, he feels 'heat in the very sod that the saints have printed!' There is great comfort in the promise of Christ's companionship, and in the Communion of Saints.

I remember, too, a vicar sent to a downtown parish where there was a vast population, much unemployment, and much mindless vandalism. The huge vicarage was hard to live in, and was too expensive to heat. A nearby factory put out foul fumes that stank as far as the borders of his parish. Since the church was poor, I don't suppose there was a paid caretaker, so I imagine the newly-appointed vicar would have to roll up his sleeves to sweep and dust the church, and light the worn-out boiler with whatever fuel he could find. Then, no doubt, he would toll the bell and wait to see who came to worship at the service of Holy Communion. A few faithful old folk would probably arrive, to sit in ones and twos in the otherwise desert of empty pews. The vicar would hear his own voice echoing in the almost empty building, but hardly hear the faint response of the few. He would feel very much alone! But then would come the *Sursum Corda*; and as he exhorted the despondent to lift up their hearts, so would his own lift in gladsome praise. 'Therefore with Angels and Archangels, *and with all the company of heaven*, we laud and magnify thy glorious name . . .'

He would realize that he was not alone, nor the worshippers few, for they had been joined with all the company of heaven. Angels and archangels joined in the paean of praise. The place was packed with the great multitude that no man could number. Heaven was all about them: *it was All Saints' Day!*

I think every day must have been All Saints' Day for him. For he stayed a brave lifetime in that parish, and never once did I hear him complain. He rejoiced in the Communion of Saints. He fostered Christian fellowship in the parish. The congregations increased, and the church was built up in the faith. How glad I was to see him ultimately move into a brand new vicarage! *Sursum Corda!* Alleluia!

If you are feeling depressed, if the burdens of life seem too heavy, if you feel on your own with no one at hand to help; then know that this is God's message to you. God has vowed never to leave us, nor forsake us; for Christ has promised to be with us always; and the holy saints ever encompass us. So get out your prayer book, read again the epistle and gospel, and say the prayer appointed for All Saints' Day. Then go to church, lift up your heart, and join with all the company of heaven in thanksgiving to God for all his mercies. Your despondency will be dispelled, your feeling of loneliness overcome, and you will find in Christ renewed strength to go on, rejoicing in the company of the blessed saints.

> O blest communion, fellowship divine!
> We feebly struggle, they in glory shine;
> Yet all are one in thee, for all are thine. Alleluia!
> (Bishop W. W. How)

REMEMBRANCE SUNDAY
Constructive Recollection

. . . a time to kill, and a time to heal . . .
ECCLESIASTES 3.3

Some have said that wars are best forgotten, that to hark back to the past does nothing but keep open the wounds. They see little value in history, and would close the book on the pain and suffering of past wars. 'Peacetime', they say, 'is the time to heal, for the time of killing is over.' Others hold a different opinion. The Psalmist was a man of peace. In former days he had fought his battles, seen senseless slaughter, and on occasion had to seek refuge from his foes. So why does he want to rake up the past and pass it on to his children, and their children, and the generations as yet unborn? A verse from one of his psalms gives the answer

> That which . . . our fathers have told us. We will not hide them from their children . . . that the generation to come might know . . . that they might set their hope in God, and not forget the works of God, but keep his commandments. (Psalm 78.3–7)

WISDOM FROM THE PAST

First, it must be said that memory is a God-given faculty and that some who have seen suffering, human nature being what it is, cannot forget. Nor should they! God gave us the ability to remember the past in order to provide hope for the future and a spur to the present. 'Those who cannot remember the past are condemned to repeat it', said Santayana. Moreover, future generations may have to go through it, again. Perhaps that is why the Bible contains as much history as exhortation.

Even so, the prime purpose of Remembrance Sunday, despite the name, is not to just to remember. It rightly recalls the comrades killed in war. It rightly honours the self-sacrifices of the slain, 'who gave their today that we might have our tomorrow' (as the Royal

British Legion likes to put it). Church parades and Cenotaph ceremonies rightly honour the men and women who fought for freedom against an evil regime. 'At the going down of the sun, and in the morning we will remember them.' We remember those who were killed or wounded in the two great World Wars, together with those who fell in the Falklands, in Northern Ireland, and in Kuwait.

But Remembrance Sunday has an even more important purpose, to pass on to posterity the costly lessons of what led up to war, why it was fought, and how such terrible catastrophes may in future be avoided.

Few veterans of the First World War are still alive to tell of the trenches, the mud, the blood, and the slaughter of so many of their comrades. Even those of us who saw service in the Second World War are now old men, and perhaps grandparents. If *we* don't tell our children and grand-children, who can? If we don't share our memory of why war, was waged and for what cause so many died, who will? If we, the surviving veterans of the wars, were to let Remembrance Sunday lapse, we would be failing not only with our comrades, but also with our children, and children's children. With us would be buried the lessons learned at such cost. With the passage of time, our medals would turn into bits of meaningless metal, and the Cenotaph seem no more than a pillar of senseless stone!

COURAGE FOR THE PRESENT

The nation of Israel is determined to make no such mistake. Down the long centuries it has suffered much. Persecution and pain and deprivation have been Israel's teachers. Suffering has drilled into the national memory the peril of forgetting the past. History is no academic exercise to the Jews. Past lessons are considered essential for future survival. As the Psalmist said, the children must know. I remember visiting Israel's monument and museum, built to remember the Jews who suffered and died in their millions during the hellish Holocaust. Of all the heart-rending exhibits, the most moving were the pathetic letters of little children torn from their parents and sent to the dreaded concentration camps. Many were exterminated in the gas-chambers, but those who survived are determined that their children must be told. The Psalmist was right! What they had learnt at such painful cost from the past must not be hidden from the future. Never again

108

must they walk as lambs to the slaughter.

Each age and generation has its own way of remembering. In the years after the silencing of the guns in 1918; at the eleventh hour, of the eleventh day, of the eleventh month, complete silence was observed throughout the nation. Sunday or weekday, all traffic was stopped. Weavers stopped their looms, factories were silenced, typewriters ceased to chatter, and people stood still in the streets. For two long minutes there was utter silence, as the past took over the present. Red poppies brought back faces from the bloody fields of Flanders, and dear ones 'loved long since, and lost awhile' were vividly recalled.

Seventy or more years on, Remembrance Day is now held on a Sunday, a yet more holy day! Memories have become even more sacred for being recalled on the day of worship. Each of us has memories which are special to us. On this day I remember my friend burnt in an aircraft on an African runway—the comrade who took my place! My memory moves to Iceland, where I saw men with incredible courage carrying their wounded aircrew across miles of razor-sharp rocks, their boots and feet cut to ribbons. Others will recall the courage of men in war-time convoys, dive-bombed or torpedoed, while they brought food to these shores. Yet others will think about army pals risking their lives that their comrades might live. All of us ex-servicemen and women alike have many brave deeds in our minds this day, and each of has his own way of commemorating the past.

HOPE FOR THE FUTURE

But on this special day we should look not only at the past with gratitude, but also towards the future with faith and hope. We are to tell our children in order, as the Psalmist says, 'That they may set their hope in God'. The tale of God's past providence inspires faith in God for the future. We are to tell of 'the works of God' that generations to come may not only speak of 'God our help in ages past', but also believe in God 'our hope for years to come'. We are to tell the next generation of the fateful days when the whole nation was called to prayer, and how God brought us through the days of peril. Tell of God's faithfulness, that future generations to come may sing his praise. Let memories of the past, and hopes of the future, strengthen our resolve to obey God, who is 'The same yesterday, today, and forever' (Hebrews 13.8).

SAINT ANDREW'S DAY (30 November)
Missionary Sunday

Jesus said follow me, and I will make you fishers of men.

MATTHEW 4.19

THE FISHERMAN

Whenever I think of St Andrew I think of Scotland. It is not just because the Scots adopted him as their Patron Saint, but because the gospels give me the impression of a Scottish fisherman, a rugged man of few words, cautious in character, level-headed, and courageous; the type of man you would like to have by your side in a storm. He was, in fact, one of the fishing fraternity, making a hard-earned living from the Sea of Galilee. The name describes the man, for Andrew is Greek for 'manly' and 'brave'. He was quiet and modest, not the type to sell himself or to push to the front. In the gospels, he seemed to stand in the shadow of his more prominent brother, Peter. Everyone in Bethsaida seemed to know of the outspoken fisherman who was always ready to take the lead; but Andrew was known only as 'Simon Peter's brother'. He was quietly content to be just a useful member of the crew. As such, he proved invaluable; always ready to lend a hand, and utterly loyal. Perhaps that was why Jesus chose him to be one of his crew of twelve disciples. The gospels say that out of the many who followed, Jesus chose twelve 'that they should be with him' (for training), 'that he might send them forth' as fishers of men (Evangelists).

THE SECOND FIDDLE

Despite his modesty, Andrew has the distinction of being the first to be chosen. To him, also, belongs the credit for bringing Peter into the faith of Christ. But for Andrew, the Christian Church might not have had Peter. It was Andrew who first found faith in Jesus as the Christ.

Although, some time later at Caesarea Philippi, Peter made his own magnificent declaration of faith in Christ, Son of the Living God (the rock on which Jesus promised to build his Church), it was Andrew who first told his brother that Jesus was the Christ.

> One of the two which heard Jesus speak, and followed him, was Andrew, Simon Peter's brother. He first findeth his own brother Simon, and saith unto him, We have found the Messiah, which is, being interpreted, the Christ. (John 1.40–41)

It says much for the loyalty and self-effacement of Andrew that he agreed to play second-fiddle to Peter. As in many families, the quieter person is pushed into the background by the more outspoken members. It probably had happened to Andrew in the home, and in the fishing partnership, and now he noticed it happening in the Church. It was he who had been first to find Christ, but now he had to stand back while Peter, James and John were brought into the inner circle of discipleship. He showed not a trace of jealousy or resentment, instead, I believe that when Peter preached with great converting power at Pentecost, Andrew was proud that his own brother was so used of God. He, himself, felt unable to preach, but he had brought to Christ one who could!

THE INVESTIGATOR

It was said of Jesus that 'he knew what was in man'. What qualities then did he discern in Andrew that made him so desirable as a disciple? The word 'caution' has been mentioned. It was a counterbalance to Peter's impulsiveness. A careless reading of the compressed account in St Mark's gospel might give the impression that the first call to Andrew and his brother to become disciples was when Jesus stood on the shore of Galilee while they were casting their nets, and that they 'straightway forsook their nets and followed him' (Mark 1.18). Oh, no! Not Andrew! He was not the type to be stampeded into a sudden decision to leave his livelihood, his precious boat and nets, at the challenge of a stranger. He was level-headed, cautious, and had in him something of the canny Scot. He was the kind of man Jesus commended as first 'counting the cost'. Reference to St John's gospel (1.35) reveals that this was by no means Andrew's first encounter with Christ, and that he had previously made a careful investigation of the so-called Messiah.

111

When John Baptist pointed to Jesus as the One who would take away the sin of the world, Andrew decided to find out more about this so-called 'Lamb of God'. When Jesus turned to see who was trailing after him and asked 'What seek ye?', Andrew and his companion replied 'Rabbi . . . where dwellest thou?' 'Come and see', or 'Come and you will see', said Jesus — for he knew it was more than mere curiosity, but rather a question of serious intent. This would be no casual visit, but an intense investigation. They did not wish to see a house, but to find out the truth about Jesus. It proved to be a life-changing experience. They stayed hour after hour, as day lengthened into night. Their questioning seemed endless. I'd dearly love to know what they asked Jesus, and what he replied; for he had the words of eternal life, and Andrew was convinced.

THE EVANGELIST

Andrew wanted to pass on the good news. Convinced of Christ, he was keen to tell others. The convert became a witness, and the first person he thought of was his own brother. 'He first findeth his own brother Simon.' He started his world mission of evangelism in the most difficult place of all — at home, and to his own family. Some young Christians want immediately to follow their conversion by going as missionaries to foreign shores. Their enthusiasm is commendable, but first let let them learn to witness at home. Let them commend Christ by their consideration and behaviour towards their nearest and dearest. Then, let them witness to those with whom they work. The Apostolic pattern was to start at the centre where they were, and then work outwards to the circumference. They began in accordance with Christ's command to witness, irst in Jerusalem, then in Judaea, then Samaria, finally going 'unto the uttermost part of the earth'. Andrew was good at personal evangelism. His method was to present people to Christ, one by one. He was approachab le, ready to listen, and quick to befriend. When a great crowd followed Jesus up the mountain far from the shops, and been so intrigued by his teaching that they had forgotten the passage of time until they felt the pangs of hunger, it was kindly Andrew to whom the little lad turned to offer his barley loaves and two small fishes. It was Jesus who wrought the mighty miracle of feeding the five thousand, but it was Andrew who put the loaves into his hands. Some with their eyes on the masses would have

112

ignored one small boy, but not Andrew! The miracle led some in the crowd to realize 'This is of a truth that prophet that should come into the world' (John 6.14). It led also to Christ's teaching on the bread of life (John 6.32 ff.). But it was ordinary Andrew, with his kindly interest in the individual, who brought these great blessings on the crowd.

On another momentous occasion, when Jerusalem was packed with pilgrims to the Passover, a few Greek visitors were standing on the edge of the crowd, and said 'Sir, we would see Jesus'. Andrew and his friend Philip introduced them to Christ. Isn't this what true evangelism is all about, not manipulating the masses; but by friendship bringing individuals to Christ?

The Pharisees, impressed by the size of the crowd, complained 'the world is gone after him' (John 12.19). But it was Andrew who realized the worth of the few foreigners to Christ. Jesus saw in them the first fruits of the mighty ingathering of the Gentiles that would follow his death (see John 12.24).

THE MISSIONARY

Was it this meeting with those Greeks that inspired Andrew to become a missionary in the land of Greece? Tradition says that he laboured mightily in Scythia and Greece, and that his fame rests upon men won for Christ and the kingdom of God. Certainly his horizons had been stretched since the day Jesus called him from Lake of Galilee, and promised to make him a fisher of men together with Peter (Mark 1.17). From being an ordinary provincial fisherman, a background figure in the gospel story, he had become a mighty missionary and emissary of Christ; taking men alive for God and his kingdom. As a bold witness, his courage and endurance were put to the severest test. He suffered martyrdom by crucifixion at Patra, near the entrance to the Gulf of Corinth. His cross was said to be diagonally shaped. It is emblazoned on Scotland's flag, and intersects the cross of St George on the Union Flag. According to the legendary story, St Andrew seeing his cross in the distance said:

Hail, Cross! which in the body of Christ wast dedicated and adorned with His members, as with pearls. Before the Lord mounted up to thee, thou didst inspire earthly fear; but now, since thou obtainest heavenly love for us, art undergone with devotion. Calm and rejoicing, therefore, come I to thee, that lifting me up, thou mayest receive me as a disciple of Him who hung upon thee . . .

Now, St Andrew is not only the Patron Saint of Scotland, and of all missionaries, but is also a constant reminder of the mighty things Christ can accomplish by ordinary folk, who dare to obey his call, and commit their lives to his service.